Berwick-upon-Tweed

A View from The Walls

John Convey

Published by John Convey
Berwick-upon-Tweed: June 2017

ISBN 978-0-9954621-1-3
Email: john@conveys.org
Graphic Design by Dan Convey: enquire@danconveys.com
Map on page 2 © OpenStreetMap contributors. ODbL 1.0
Printed by Martins the Printers, Berwick-upon-Tweed

Copyright © John Convey 2017

The moral right of John Convey to be identified as the author of this work has been asserted by him in accordance with the Copyright, Designs and Patents Act 1988.

Any profits from the sale of this book will be donated to charity

To the Memory of

Margaret Ramsay of Southport

- An Inspiration

Acknowledgements

I would like to thank the following for their help: Linda Bankier, Archivist at the Berwick Record Office, not only for advice and providing sources but also for reading through a draft of the book and making many useful suggestions; the staff at the Berwick Record Office, Berwick Library, Berwick Museum and Art Gallery, Northumberland Archives at Woodhorn, National Library of Scotland in Edinburgh and the National Archives at Kew. I thank my wife Eileen, Ged and Caroline Convey and Jane McQueen for reading the draft and suggesting improvements.

Many thanks must go to my son Dan for his help, advice and above all the design of the book.
The following were kind enough to allow me to publish my photographs taken on their property: Alison Douglas, Trust Administrator for the Berwick Preservation Trust, for the interior of the Bank Hill Ice House; and English Heritage for the interior of The Magazine and exteriors of the properties for which they are responsible, including the walls themselves.
Every effort has been made to ensure that all copyright holders have been contacted and agree to images being reproduced; we apologise if we have made any errors on this count, and will endeavour to correct these in any future edition.

Disclaimer

The information herein is given in good faith and is believed to be accurate at the time of publication. No responsibility is accepted by the author or publisher for any omissions or errors, nor for any loss or injury howsoever caused. Please take extra care when walking around the walls of Berwick - there are steep drops in several places.
The publisher would welcome any corrections which could be incorporated in any future edition.

CONTENTS

Section	Page
Map	2
Introduction	3
1 Longstone View and Pier	4
2 The Old Smoke House and Cleet Court	8
3 Ness Street	10
4 The Old Grammar School and view towards Spittal	13
5 The Avenue	15
6 Fisher's Fort	18
7 Governor's House and Gardens	21
8 Palace Green	23
9 Views from Coxon's Tower	26
10 St Aidan's House, and view of the three bridges	28
11 Wellington Terrace	30
12 The Main Guard	32
13 Quay Walls Nos 19-23	34
14 The Custom House, 18 Quay Walls	36
15 The Chandlery, and Quay Walls Nos 15-17	38
16 Sandgate	40
17 Quay Walls Nos 10-14	43
18 Quay Walls Nos 8-9, Bridge Street	45
19 Berwick YHA, Dewar's Lane	48
20 Quay Walls Nos 6-7, Quayside Look-Out	50
21 Quay Walls Nos 3-5	52
22 Quay Walls Nos 1-2	54

Section	Page
23 Berwick Bridge	56
24 Bridge End	59
25 Bridge Terrace and Love Lane	62
26 Royal Tweed Bridge	65
27 Ice House, Leaping Salmon	68
28 Bank Hill	70
29 Meg's Mount views and Royal Border Bridge	73
30 Marygate	77
31 Castlegate	81
32 Greenside Avenue	83
33 Infirmary, and Violet Terrace	85
34 Hatters' Lane	87
35 College Place	89
36 Coxon's Lane	91
37 Wallace Green	93
38 Looking back along the walls, and the Churchyard	96
39 From Brass Bastion	98
40 Church of Holy Trinity and St Mary	101
41 Cowport	103
42 The Barracks	105
43 Views, Windmill Bastion	108
44 The Magazine	110
45 Lions House and Allotments	112
46 Kings Mount, and back to Ness Gate	114
Sources	117
Index	121

A SELECTION OF VIEWPOINTS ALONG THE WALK

- **1** LONGSTONE VIEW AND PIER
- **7** GOVERNOR'S HOUSE & GARDENS
- **12** THE MAIN GUARD
- **16** SANDGATE
- **23** BERWICK BRIDGE
- **29** MEG'S MOUNT
- **30** MARYGATE
- **33** INFIRMARY, AND VIOLET TERRACE
- **37** WALLACE GREEN
- **40** CHURCH OF HOLY TRINITY AND ST MARY
- **42** BARRACKS
- **45** LIONS HOUSE AND ALLOTMENTS

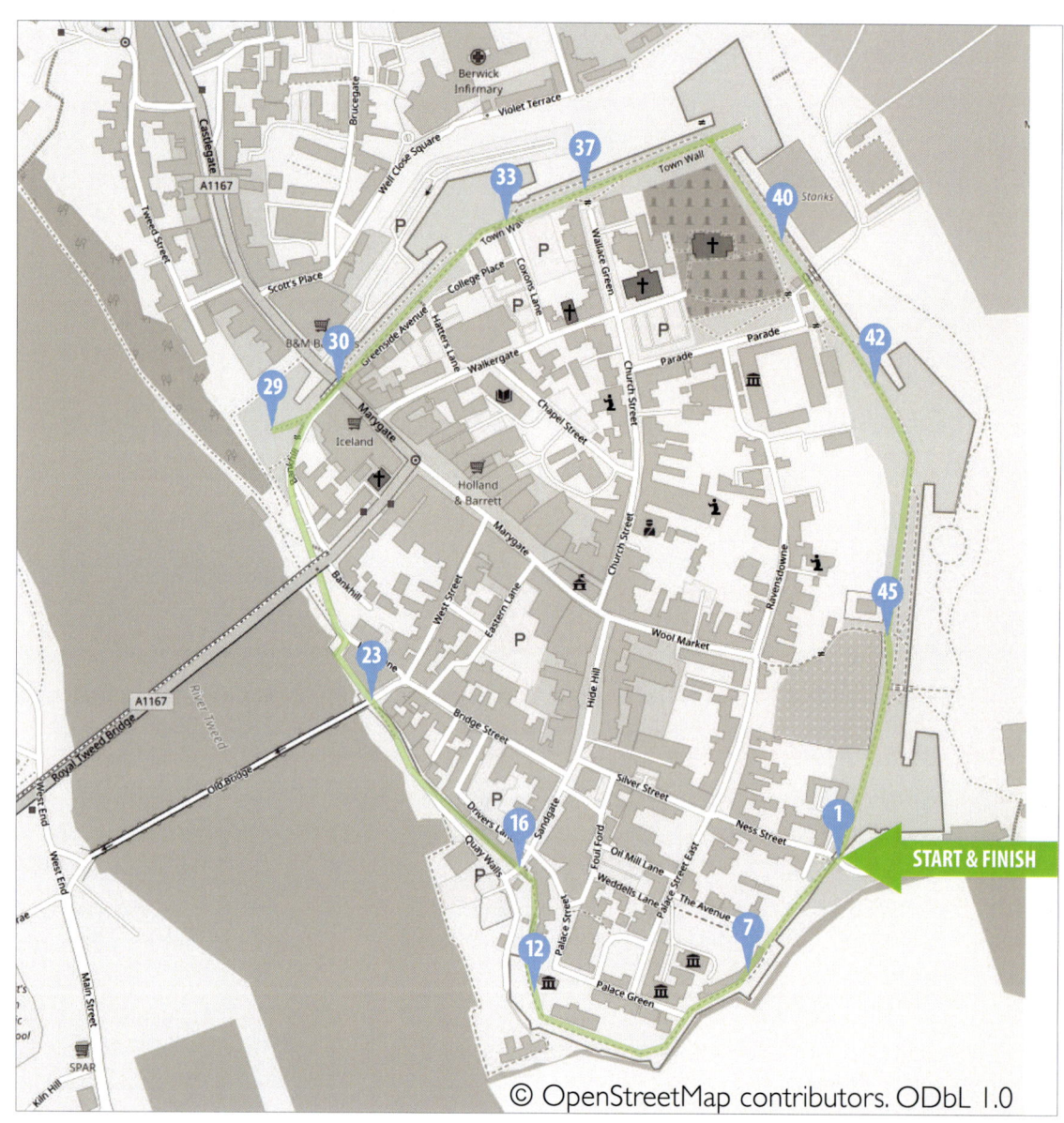

INTRODUCTION

This book is a photographic, descriptive and historical view of Berwick-upon-Tweed as seen from the town's surviving walls. It aims to show how Berwick-upon-Tweed 'looked' at a particular point in time; the 'view' is from a circuit of the surviving walls and ramparts, a distance of approximately 1.3 miles (2.13 km). When 'Google Street' has moved on to show only the latest images, one of the intentions of this book is to stand as a view of the town in 2015, to help answer the question from future generations: "but what did it look like in 2015?".

It is definitely 'A' view of Berwick, certainly not 'The' view; other authors would have different approaches.

All the photographs (apart from three) were taken in the year 2015 - the year Berwick-upon-Tweed celebrated 900 years of its written history; two of the three images illustrate later events not to be missed - the beacon lit on Windmill Bastion on the occasion of the Queen's 90th birthday, 21 April 2016 and the Flying Scotsman crossing the Royal Border Bridge on 14 May 2016.

Accompanying the photographs are descriptions of the buildings and structures, and a framework of their histories, leaving readers to embellish this framework with their own further research using the list of sources and/or their own knowledge and experience of the town.

One might get the impression that nothing changes in so old and enclosed a conservation area within and close to the walls, but several 'developments' have taken place in the short time between when the photographs were taken and the completion of the supporting text.

There were at least six obvious developments to buildings or sites over just a few months: Governor's Gardens, St Aidan's School near Wellington Terrace, William Cowe's shop at the foot of West Street, the new eco-houses on Bank Hill, the old KwikSave site on Walkergate and the refurbishment of the play park in the stanks between Windmill Bastion and King's Mount; and in the pipeline are the redevelopment of the old cinema site on Sandgate and the new hospital on the Infirmary site….will the Bell Tower still be there in 2020?

The comments about buildings are the author's own, informed by using listed building websites and sources such as Pevsner's *Northumberland* (Buildings of England Series)[40] and the many other sources found at the end of this book. The author is not an architect so on occasion may get his rusticated quoins mixed up with his Tuscan pilasters!

WARNING. This is not intended to be a guide that you read as you walk around the walls, rather one that you read at home before or afterwards. If you do read it while on the walls, always be aware that there are steep sides to the walls in places and it is very dangerous to approach the edge; and please keep the children to the paths and well away from the edges. After all, the walls were built to keep out the enemy of the day! There is a handy guide *Walking the Walls*[55] produced by the Berwick-upon-Tweed Civic Society which is easy to read and carry around, but still do take care!

1 LONGSTONE VIEW AND PIER

LONGSTONE VIEW, BLACK WATCH TOWER AND WALLS

Looking seawards from above Ness Gate, in the foreground is Longstone View built in the first decade of the twentieth century, with its 'hanging gardens of Berwick' clinging to the ancient walls; behind it are the restored and improved Edwardian walls around King's Mount, including the round Black Watch Tower. In the mid-nineteenth century this area was a timber yard, and an earlier map of 1816 shows four limekilns. The buildings of Longstone View are substantial three-storey houses, faced with random-sized stones and with plain door cases and fanlights. On a clear day, and with very good eyesight, Longstone lighthouse on the Farne Islands can be seen from here.

'Ness Gate', sometimes also called 'Pier Gate', was burrowed through

NESS GATE FROM PIER ROAD

the walls around 1810 to give access to the new Pier Road and the pier which was under construction at the time - in the Guild Minutes for 10 June 1811: "Mr Marshall moved that the road leading to the shore through Ness Gate be put into repair by Committee of Works….".[8] In his *History of Berwick-upon-Tweed* published in 1799, Fuller had previously suggested a gate here would be an 'improvement': "If a Sally Port were opened in the walls in a line with Silver Street, it would be productive of much convenience to all the inhabitants in the under part of the town, as it would afford a new road for their servants to carry out their clothes to dry on the shore. It would also be advantageous to the public by opening a much nearer and better road to the lime kilns and those parts of the shore where sea ware is thrown out".[45]

> "An initial ceremony took place in February 1810, with great ringing of bells and processions from church to the pier site under the gaze of "an immense concourse of people"."

On King's Mount itself, behind Longstone View, a block of nine houses was built prior to 1897 as 'Married Quarters' for soldiers from the Barracks. By 1968 there was only one house in occupation, and the houses were later demolished.

The pier snaking out to sea was completed nearly 200 years ago. A pier did exist before the present one, built in the reign of Elizabeth I, between April 1577 and April 1580; at that time, some of the cost headings included: 'chief officers, hardhewers, quarrymen, barrowmen, labourers, carriages, smiths, carpenters, sawyers, coble hire, boys, baring the quarry at St Cuthbert's well, thatching the masons' lodges at Salterspith and St Cuthbert's well, freights, sounding the haven, &c'.[11] The total cost of the construction of the Elizabethan pier was £1112 8s. 10¼d. As with any structure battered by the sea, it required regular repair; but by Fuller's time, around 1799, it was in need of rebuilding: a pier 'would greatly widen and deepen the bed of the river as also the harbour mouth. Ships could sail in or out on any wind'.[45]

On 18 June 1808, the Royal Assent was given for 'An Act for rebuilding the Pier and for improving the Harbour of Berwick-upon-Tweed'. An initial ceremony took place in Feb 1810, with great ringing of bells and processions from church to the pier site under the gaze of "an immense concourse of people".[71]

To facilitate the transport of stone for the pier, a Berwick Pier Railway, a horse-drawn waggonway, was constructed along the coast from the quarry at Spittal to a jetty from where it was transported across the estuary; the jetty appears to be east of Carr Rock, behind what is now the premises of the Multi Fuel Stove Company.[61]

The present pier, designed by John Rennie, was completed around 1825 at a cost of £61,536. The lighthouse was added in 1826, the foundation stone being laid in February that year; the lighthouse was designed by Joseph Nelson. For many years in the nineteenth century the Wilson family were the lighthouse keepers; James Wilson was also an artist and portrait painter in his spare time and was responsible for carving the statue of 'Jimmy Strength' which stood in Palace Green for many years (See Section 8).

2 THE OLD SMOKE HOUSE AND CLEET COURT

CLEET COURT AND THE OLD SMOKE HOUSE

Looking inland and north from above Ness Gate is seen The Old Smoke House, a mid-eighteenth century building now converted into a house; in 1852 it is shown as forming part of a quadrangle of buildings on the site which included a Smoking House (the building in view), a Cooperage and a 'Manufactory (Whiting)'. The aroma of smoke and herring wafting over the walls is long gone, but the name of the hill (Kipper Hill) leading up to the building is a reminder of the days when an industry of the humble kipper thrived in Berwick. In 1871, nine months with hard labour was the punishment for Samuel Johnston who stole a barrel of herrings from 'Mr Beveridge's herring yard',[71] the owner of the herrings at the time being James Gilroy; later that century the owners were the Sayers. Being an industrial building, the stonework has rough finish with random-sized blocks, the roof using the distinctive traditional pantiles.

The modern flats and houses of Cleet Court are built on land formerly used in the nineteenth century as a timber yard; the site also housed a granary and drying kiln. After that it had various uses, including a Sports Centre shop in 1940s, and latterly a builder's yard until 1986, when Cleet Court, comprising 23 houses and flats, was built. At least the pantiles on the roofs of Cleet Court are in harmony with surrounding older properties, even if much else is not. Currently, a planning application has been permitted to replace the external windows and doors with new woodgrain effect UPVC double glazed units; part of the Case Officer's response is: "although the building is subject to statutory protection afforded by the Conservation Area/Article 4 Direction, the style of fenestration treatments currently are not in keeping with the local vernacular and therefore not in the spirit of the objectives of the Article 4. As such the recommendation is for approval of the application subject to a condition that the proposed replacement units replicate the pattern and form of the existing openings".[41]

3 NESS STREET

BAY TERRACE, NESS STREET

NESS STREET FROM ABOVE NESS GATE

Looking towards town from above Ness Gate is seen Ness Street: "Ness Street is one of the most evocative of the narrower streets, a tiny route squeezed with ancient cottages and with a tantalizingly blank view of the North Sea horizon framed through Ness Gate at the end". [30]

From just below Ness Street down to the river, and including Palace Street and surrounds, is a flat area of land which from at least medieval times was called the Ness, meaning a promontory or headland. A medieval palace existed on the Ness, as did a Carmelite friary founded in 1270. The area was included within the walls constructed by Edward I, but in the initial plans for the Elizabethan fortifications it was left at the mercy of the river, the sea, the Scots and the French below the Cat Well Wall stretching between what is now King's Mount and Meg's Mount. This is illustrated by the map entitled *The True Description of Her Majesties Town of Barwick* from around 1580 in the British Library which shows a birds-eye view (forerunner of Google Earth?) of the town with each individual building shown, complete with windows, roofs, doors and individual gardens with fencing. Before the Elizabethan fortifications were completed, however, the idea of the Cat Well Wall (or Cat Wall) was abandoned.[60] The Edwardian wall around the Ness was repaired and strengthened, and the Ness was reprieved.

Nicholas Pevsner, in the Northumberland edition of his series *The Buildings of England*, missed a gem in Ness Street, as his 'perambulations' skirted both ends but mentioned it not. The housing is mainly eighteenth century Georgian with simpler architecture than the grand Georgian buildings of Ravensdowne or Quay Walls, but nevertheless full of atmosphere and history with its narrow street and slightly leaning facades. The view from the Ravensdowne end, taking in the narrow street and the arch of Ness Gate with the pier and sea beyond, is one of the iconic views of Berwick.[40]

Houses numbered 2-20 on the left are eighteenth century, as are No 5 and probably No 7 on the right. They have the distinctive red pantiles on the roofs, brick chimneys, largely brightly coloured rendering, and simple window and doorway surrounds. No 14 is quite different, with three storeys, a pedimented doorway and wooden cornice; the ground floor front room acted as a sweet shop for some years in the last century. On the right side, quaint No 5 has a Doric door surround with Tuscan pillars, an open pediment and wonky fanlight. No 7 is faced with rougher stone, and has simple doorway and window surrounds. At the far end, beyond No 2, on the corner with Palace Street East, is the early nineteenth century former Ness Gate Hotel [Ravensdowne House], now converted into private flats. It has a pedimented doorway with pilasters and simple fanlight. If you look closely, the outline of the former hotel's name can be seen on the front. In its days as a hotel it also acquired 2-10 Ness Street, but the houses returned to separate units around 1993.

The modern buildings on the right foreground, Cleet Court, were built in 1986 on a former builders' yard (see Section 2 above). A photograph taken around 1903 shows a high wall separating the timber yard from the street; some of this wall has been retained, although not to the original height.[7]

> " Ness Street is one of the most evocative of the narrower streets. "

The two huge houses of Bay Terrace, with their imposing chimney stacks, were built later than 2-20 Ness Street, in the early nineteenth century; they seem to be shown on Wood's map of 1822. The door surrounds are more elaborate, but some of the sash windows have been altered over time. Benjamin George Sinclair had been living at No 1 Bay Terrace for some years before his death in 1912. He was a busy man: his list of occupations included insurance agent, ship broker, timber merchant (with office and yard in Ness Street), and the grandest title of all: 'Vice-Consul for France, Denmark, Sweden, Norway, Italy and Belgium'! James Sinclair, his father, was the agent (his office being in Ness Street) when the wreck of the *Forfarshire* (of Grace Darling fame) and the materials saved from it were sold by auction at North Sunderland in October 1838.

THE OLD GRAMMAR SCHOOL, AND VIEW TOWARDS SPITTAL

4

THE OLD GRAMMAR SCHOOL AND YARD AT 5 PALACE STREET EAST

The Grammar School moved from Golden Square to 5 Palace Street East, an existing large mid-eighteenth century Georgian town house, in 1866; prior to that the house's garden was surrounded by trees and it boasted a fishpond. As soon as it became the Grammar School an extension was built for a chapel, opened 23 September 1867, in the Gothic style, and at the end of the nineteenth century another extension for science classrooms (on the right side of the photo on the previous page). Temporary buildings were constructed in the

OLD GRAMMAR SCHOOL YARD AND REAR OF NESS STREET

yard: in 1908 an iron and wood technical classroom and cycle store, and in 1920 a converted army hut with two classrooms; both 'temporary' buildings remain today - they were still in use when the Youth & Community Centre, which took over the building in 1951, closed its doors in 2015!

The school moved out in 1939, but the site was destined to remain as a place where young people could meet and learn and on 23 April 1951 it was officially opened as a Youth & Community Centre, at a cost of £2,230. The previous month the Berwick Advertiser included a piece on the Centre: "…we are not ostriches, and do not duck the inescapable fact that boys will meet girls, by putting our heads in the sand, but how much better is it for a boy to meet a girl in the healthy atmosphere of the centre than in the doorway on a public street?

The centre is non-sectarian and the only condition of entry is that the applicant belongs to a Youth Club. Twenty-four clubs are represented at the Centre…". The centre included "a main hall, where classes in physical training, drama, ballroom dancing etc are held; a canteen, where prices are as low as possible; a lounge, crafts room and library".(71) A canteen assistant here in 1955 earned 2/5d an hour!

The Youth and Community Centre, which latterly had also been used for adult learning, closed finally in the summer of 2015. The whole site is currently unoccupied and looking unkempt, but there are plans afoot for it to continue to serve the young people of the area.

The view towards the south includes the lone chimney at Spittal Point; this is all that remains from an area that was a hive of industrial activity in the past - in the 1920s the promontory on the south side of the Tweed boasted chemical works, gas works, manure works and a lifeboat house. Now the area is a pleasatnt walk connected to the long and wide promenade in Spittal. The name Spittal derives from the medieval leper hospital of St Bartholomew which was founded before 1234 and which is thought to have ceased early in the sixteenth century. The land eventually became Spittal Hall Farm. There is a representation of what Spittal may have looked like in medieval times in Jim Walker's book *Berwick-upon-Tweed through time*.(25) Moving away from the estuary up-river towards Tweedmouth, there are commercial buildings and the church behind Main Street and, as the

VIEW FROM ABOVE NESS GATE

ground rises beyond the caravan park and main line railway, the Highcliffe Estate can be seen climbing to the brow. From this vantage point on the walls one can also see, on the far side of the river, the Lifeboat House (see section 9 and page 115) and the abandoned railway viaduct.

THE AVENUE 5

THE RETREAT, THE AVENUE (WITH INSET)

THE AVENUE

The Avenue, situated on The Ness below Ness Street, has been inhabited for centuries - houses were shown on the street around 1580. There were three houses in 1822 - Major Forster on the corner with Palace Street East, Captain Forster mid-way along and Mr Ridpath at what is now No 6, The Retreat.

House numbers 3 and 5 are early nineteenth century; the unusual red brick house, The Retreat, is an earlier eighteenth century building (1749 on the gate). One of the town's 'Rope Walks' is shown on old maps along the left side of the Avenue, near its boundary with Governor's Gardens; Thomas Simpson was a rope-maker in Palace Street in 1828.

LOOKING TOWARDS GOVERNOR'S GARDENS, WITH THE RETREAT ON THE RIGHT

The front of No 1 The Avenue faces Palace Street East; it has plain sash windows, and slate roof. No 3 The Avenue, Lynwood House, is early nineteenth century Georgian, faced with stone and with a pantiled roof, and doorway with fanlight in a plain frame. No 5 The Avenue, Flagstaff House, is also Georgian, with huge gable ends which rise above the first floor and hide the chimneys. It boasts a steep-sided Mansard roof in slate, with three tall dormer windows at the front and two at the rear, where there is also a tall, round-headed window with lancet design, similar to No 1 Wellington Terrace and the Zion Chapel on Bank Hill. No 6 The Avenue, *The Retreat*, is unusual in that it was built of brick in the middle of the eighteenth century, the original building using English Bond style brickwork. This building was a school in the early part of the twentieth century - Mr Paterson's School for Boys and Youths which gave "a sound education suited to the Civil Service, Medical Preliminary and other Public Examinations and especially adapted for Commercial and Scientific Pursuits".[71]

No 4 Palace St East, at the far end of The Avenue, is eighteenth century, with cast-iron balconies added later; it is rendered, with prominent quoins. Over one of the windows is a shield of the arms of the Call family. Next door, No 6 Palace Street East, is eighteenth or early nineteenth century, rendered, with prominent quoins and the door surround with Corinthian columns.

THE AVENUE LOOKING TOWARDS PALACE STREET EAST

A Carmelite Friary, probably founded in 1270, was said to be located in the Ness, close to the later Governor's House. *The True Description of Her Majesties Town of Barwick* map of around 1580 shows a few prominent buildings (e.g. Holy Trinity Church) with roofs coloured grey, as if covered by slate; there was a group of such buildings in the Ness, which may have been those of the former Carmelite Friary, dissolved about 40 years earlier; or more likely the medieval Palace (see Section 8) after which the street was named. Archaeological investigations in 2001 found medieval stonework below ground, but there was insufficient evidence to conclude that it formed part of the Friary, or Palace.[60]

6 FISHER'S FORT

VIEW FROM FISHER'S FORT LOOKING SOUTH

FISHER'S FORT

CAPTURED RUSSIAN GUN

'Fisher's Fort' was constructed before the Elizabethan fortifications on the line of the Edwardian walls, and improved in later centuries. It sports a cannon captured during the Crimean War. This 'trophy of war' was offered to the town in May 1858; the inhabitants provided the money for a cast-iron gun carriage. The gun was delivered by sea in January 1859 - 'it is 13 cwt in weight, it is 7 feet 2 inches long, and it is stated to be an 18 pounder'.[71] It wasn't until August 1861 that the gun was placed on the walls, initially surrounded by railings.

Looking towards the pier from 'Fisher's Fort', Pier Road was constructed around 1810 to give better access to the new pier which was in the course of construction. In the Guild Minutes of 10 June 1811, 'Mr Marshall moved that the road leading to the shore through Ness Gate be put into repair by Committee of Works....[8]' Johnstone, writing in 1817, wrote that this road, and the new road along the

19

bays, with a 'kiln house' on the east end; by 1874 a new kiln had been added at the west end. It remained a maltings until the early 1930s, when it was occupied by William Leith, sailmakers and tentmakers, for many years. In the recent conversion to residential accommodation, the pyramid-shaped roofs of the malt kilns at the east and west ends have been preserved.

VIEW FROM FISHER'S FORT TOWARDS PIER ROAD

> " Berwick's whaling industry lasted from about 1807 until 1838, when the last whaler, the *Norfolk*, was sold. "

river towards the castle, were 'lately finished'.[47] It is possible to see the remains of what could have been a cobbled road leading from the sands up to the beginning of the Pier Road.

On the photo above, on the left on Pier Road is Longstone View, (see Section 1) and immediately beyond Longstone View is the converted Maltings, part of which had previously been a whale oil house. Before the discovery of mineral oil, whale oil had many uses, including as a lubricant, for lighting and in industries such as woollen cloth, sailmaking, tanning, soap and metalworking, and a basic ingredient of paints and varnishes.[33] Berwick's whaling industry lasted from about 1807 until 1838, when the last whaler, the *Norfolk*, was sold. As she arrived home in May 1837 she was welcomed by crowds of residents. The ship was 309 tons, built in 1793, and the Master at that time was George Harrison. John M Dixon was the manager of the Berwick Whale Fishing Co in 1829 and lived in Wellington Terrace. Around 1838 the whale oil house was converted into a maltings and by 1852 the Pier Road Malt House had been extended from eight to thirteen

On the rise behind Pier Road is Devon Terrace, built 1897-98, and beyond that the Coastguard Cottages (See Section 46). Further along the road is the former Harbour Commissioners Storehouse, now a private house under renovation. The Harbour Commissioners were established in 1808 to oversee the building of the new pier and harbour improvements; the Berwick-upon-Tweed Harbour Commission still exists and is the owner of the present docks in Tweedmouth.

A church, named after St Nicholas, the Patron Saint of Sailors, stood on or behind Pier Road, with the churchyard extending back as far as what is now the cricket ground. One of the towers on the medieval wall near King's Mount was called "St Nicholas' Tower" and stood roughly at the top of the present steps from Pier Road.

GOVERNOR'S HOUSE & GARDENS   7

NEW HOUSING DEVELOPMENT IN THE FORMER GARDENS

The surviving Governor's House, built for the military Governor of Berwick, dates from 1719-1720, and was designed most likely by the architect of the Barracks, Nicholas Hawksmoor. Previously there had been a 'Governor's lodging' in the area - in 1595 "The breach in the old town wall next Tweed behind the Governor's lodging, now fallen, to be done with hewn stone from the foundation, will cost £73".[11] In June 1718 the Board of Ordnance requested that Captain Phillips, the engineer in charge of building the Barracks, prepare an estimate for building a new house for the Governor of Berwick. The old house was to be demolished, and the new one to use any timber left over from the Barracks. The estimate for the building was £544 8s 10d, with an additional £103 1s 8d in July 1719, when the project was finally approved.

A map of 1725 shows 'The Governor's House and Gardens'; shortly after, in Buck's view of the 1740s the House had just two storeys, but by 1799 a third storey had been added, and Fuller's map of that year has an illustration of the house and neatly laid out gardens with many trees; the author describes "...a neat garden of the richest soil belongs to it".[45]

It ceased to be the Governor's residence around 1837 and the eight-bedroomed house was for sale in 1839, along with "the large garden, stable and coach-house attached".[71] The premises was used as a school and later by the Tweed Brewery - some of its buildings have been preserved and converted to private housing units. The remainder of the garden area was a timber yard in the mid-nineteenth century.

NEW HOUSING DEVELOPMENT

As regards the breweries on the site, there have been many takeovers and changes of name since 1847 - Carr & Co, Tweed Brewery, Johnson & Darlings, Border Breweries Ltd, Berwick Breweries and Vaux Brewery; these operations on the Governor's Gardens site closed down in the late 1950's.[20] Prior to Lindisfarne Homes Ltd developing the old pottery buildings and the gardens, the site was owned from the 1980s by Holy Island's Lindisfarne Ltd, who had a Wine and Spirit Museum, cafe, pottery and craft shop until the turn of the century.

The Governor's House itself is not part of Lindisfarne Homes' development. Today (May 2017) with the construction of the new houses complete and the site landscaped, it has reverted to being the "neat garden" of Fuller's day. The view from the walls shows the rear of the house - the front faces Palace Green.

PALACE GREEN 8

REAR VIEW OF BOWER VILLA, PALACE GREEN

The names Palace Street and Palace Green derive from a medieval Palace in the area. In 1586-87 "A piece of the old wall at the south west side of the palace or victual office, is ready to fall, and over-hangeth so that the people are afraid to pass over it, and is dangerous for the night watch who stand thereon—it is 100 feet long, 10 thick, and 26 high, and should be 12 feet high of hewn stone, for the better defence of the "surgies of the sea," beating on it every tide, and will cost 240l". As a victuals office for the military, it stored wheat, rye, meal, malt, 6 oxen, kyne, wethers, butter, and island cod.[11] James II considered repairing the chapel in the palace in 1688: a contract was drawn up for the 'repair of the Chapell at Berwick' amounting to £97, the chapel being 23 yards long and 7 yards wide and the roof covered with slate. It is not entirely clear whether this refers to the chapel in the old palace in Palace Green or the new Palace which had been built inside the Castle in the early seventeenth century.[17]

Immediately on the right on Palace Green (see photo on previous page) are the recently converted buildings of the former Tweed Brewery, part of the Governor's Gardens development.

NO 3 PALACE GREEN, FORMERLY BAY VIEW

It is worth a short walk down to the Green itself; Pevsner wrote that "Palace Green is a delicious oasis of old dark trees surrounded by dignified buildings".(40) The building on the Green itself is the Scout Hall, probably built around 1811 as a Reading Room; by 1858 it was called the *Subscription Reading Room, Billiard Room and Bowling Green*. The Rooms closed around October 1914 "…in consequence of falling away of membership and other causes…".(7) The scouts took over the lease of the building and their first meeting in the new premises was in December 1914. Each scout contributed 'one penny monthly for the privileges of the new quarters'.(71)

Previously, in 1895, the Reading Room had been extended to include a 'Smoking Room' at the west end, with an intricately-glazed bay window, which matched the larger bay at the front of the existing Reading Room; the Smoking Room bay still exists, but the front of the Reading Room has been slightly extended at some stage since and the bay sadly demolished. The grassed area in front of the building was formerly a bowling green which reputedly dates back to the eighteenth century.

Looking from the walls, on the left side, beyond No 3 Palace Green, is Bower Villa, an early nineteenth century house, with a coloured bust of Wellington over the doorway.

No 3 Palace Green, named Bay View until the early 1950s and currently The Old Whaling House, is early nineteenth century. The balcony at ground floor level gives access from the walls to the front door, with the basement windows being smaller than those above. At the rear is a previous carriage entrance. Further along on the left is the abandoned St Aidan's House (see Section 10).

'Jimmy Strength', whose real name was James Stuart, made many claims: to be one of the royal Stuarts; to be strong enough to lift a table with his teeth or 13 cwt from the ground or a cart full of hay; to be 115/116 years old when he died in 1844; to have taken part in many battles (including Culloden), from 1740s; to have married four (or six?) times and had 27 children; and to have played the violin - many people thought very badly! He was buried in Tweedmouth cemetery in 1844. A statue was made soon afterwards, the sculptor being James Wilson, also the lighthouse keeper. This statue stood for many years on Palace Green, but collapsed in 1953; it was hoped to restore it but unfortunately it didn't survive, the pieces that remain being stored currently in Berwick Museum.

9 VIEWS FROM COXON'S TOWER

VIEW TOWARDS TWEEDMOUTH DOCKS

Coxon's Tower (at various times called 'Bulwark in the Sands', Cockson's Tower, Palace Tower) has a basement dating back to the time of Edward I in the early fourteenth century; the rib vaulting in the roof can be seen through the small gateway. The upper part of the tower has been rebuilt and altered over the years.

Looking from Coxon's Tower, the complex of buildings on the Quay in the foreground - the Marlin buildings - includes a Customs Watch House (on the left corner), listed as recently as 2012; Marlin House, an Art Studio, the Old Lifeboat House, and the Old Lifeboat Cottage.

Looking very forlorn and unloved at the moment, the Customs Watch House, ideally situated for keeping an eye on shipping movements at the mouth of the river, is eighteenth century according to a lease dated May 1801 in the Berwick Archives which shows the building had been used by His Majesty's Customs for 'many years past'; it seems not to have appeared on maps until the 1850s. As can be seen, previously it has had other buildings attached to it, on the east and north sides, which were demolished in the last century.

The old Lifeboat House, in the centre of the buildings to the north of the Customs Watch House, was built in 1901-2 when the lifeboat moved from Spittal. As well as housing the lifeboat, there was accommodation for the crew and helpers on the first floor. The lifeboat, the *John and Janet*, was housed in the new lifeboat house by May 1902. The other buildings on either side of the original lifeboat house were built in subsequent years. This lifeboat house was replaced in 1940/1 by the new lifeboat house at Carr Rock across the river in Tweedmouth. The lifeboat at the time, the *J. and W.*, moved into the new lifeboat house at Carr Rock on 22 April 1941.[71][66]

POST-MEDIEVAL GRAFFITI ON COXON'S TOWER

The area of the Quay from the Marlin Buildings back towards The Chandlery is largely undeveloped, with the Berwick-upon-Tweed Conservation Area report using poetry to describe it: "In this respect, the southern half of the Quayside is perhaps a theatre stage, its handsome set in place but without, yet, confirmation of the players that will populate it, and the play they will create".[30]

Looking over the river one can see the Tweedmouth Docks built 1872-1876; they are still in use today, large cargo ships weaving their way round the mouth of the river and trying to avoid hitting the pier, which does happen occasionally! The docks were opened officially on 4th October 1876.

27

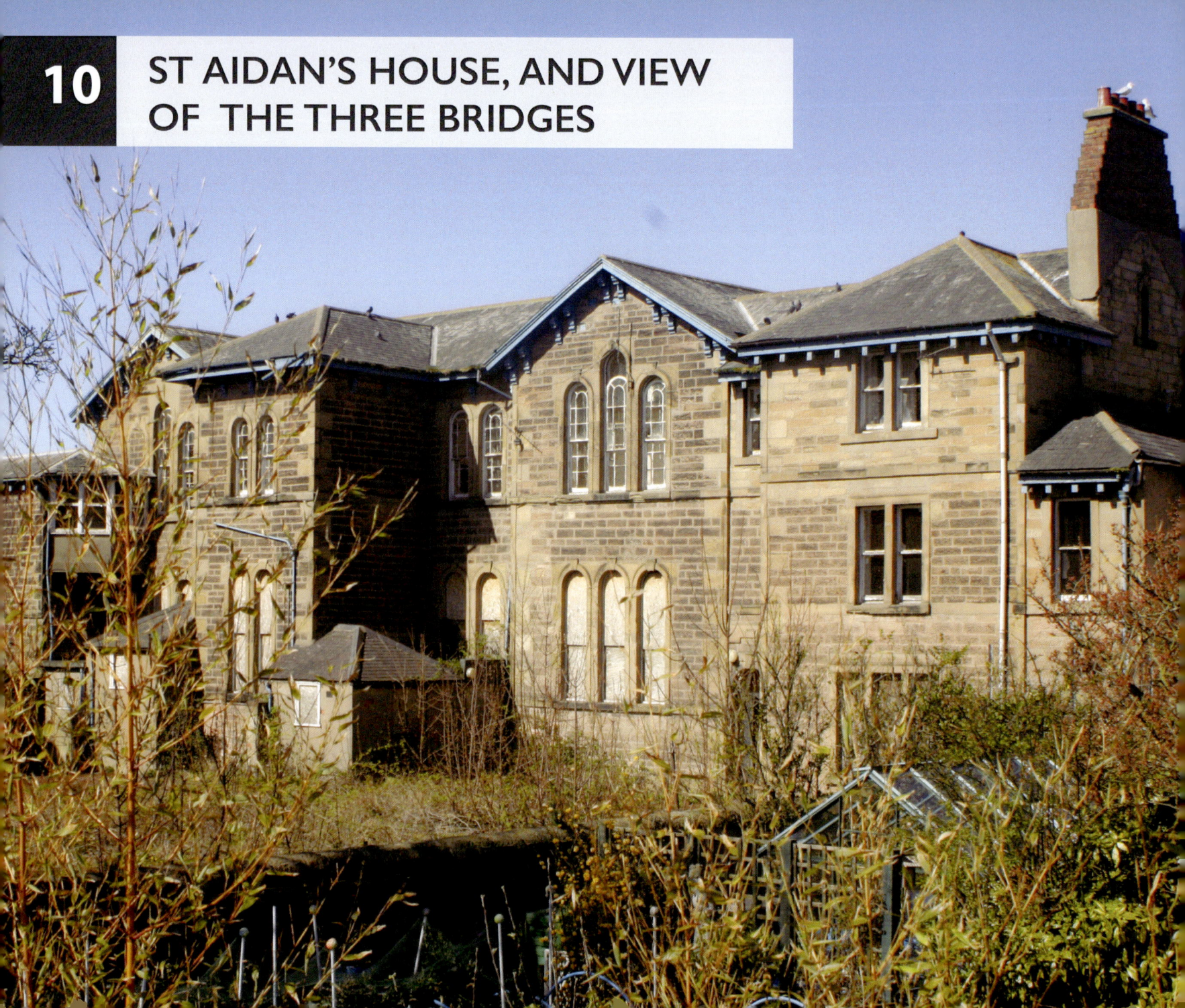

10 ST AIDAN'S HOUSE, AND VIEW OF THE THREE BRIDGES

VIEW OF THE THREE BRIDGES FROM THE SALUTING BATTERY

There was a subscription 'School of Industry' on the site of St Aidan's House in 1852; this school for girls was established in 1819, under the patronage of the ladies of Berwick for the education of poor girls. There were about 106 girls in the school in 1828, under the watchful eye of the Mistress, Emily Stirling.

The present building, known locally as 'The British School', dates from 1858-9, when the non-conformist British and Foreign School Society established schools, one for girls on the upper floor and one for boys on the ground floor; the former School of Industry was incorporated in the new schools. In May 1858 it was decided that the site for 'new subscription schools' was to be the School of Industry, Palace Green; the existing buildings were razed and new buildings erected. At either end of the main building there was a residence for the teachers.

Building commenced early in July 1858, and was completed by April 1859, with the school opening on Monday 9th May 1859. The first Inspection Report that autumn considered that 'both schools are well conducted and the general progress made in the three months since opening is very satisfactory', with about 200 girls and 200 boys attending.[71]

On ceasing to be a school, the building was converted to a hostel for Holy Island children in 1975; they needed somewhere to stay during the week while they attended school in Berwick. It accommodated twenty children, with dormitories, common study room, dining and recreation area, offices, staff accommodation, and sick bay. It has been unoccupied for about 20 years and is currently in a poor state of repair.

The building has slender, round-headed windows with prominent keystones, and quoins of rough sandstone. In 2012 planning permission was sought and granted to convert the building into residential accommodation; the building is not listed. Revised plans in November 2016 are for four 2-bedroomed units and two 3-bedroomed units, retaining much of the existing facades.

11 WELLINGTON TERRACE

Of the three grand classical houses on Wellington Terrace, Nos 1 & 2 were built around the time of Waterloo, not appearing on a map of 1816 but shown on Wood's map of 1822. No 3 was added around 1852 as the Manse for the Presbyterian Church in Golden Square; the church moved a few years later to the new building in Wallace Green. The 1852 Board of Health map shows Number 3 built, but the garden not laid out, suggesting that it was newly built. According to Macewen, the minister John Cairns moved into the property in June 1852.[76] The Vicar of the Parish Church was living next door at No 2. One wonders if they chatted amicably over the garden fence; Macewen wrote that their relationship was "quiet and friendly"! No 3 is still called 'The Manse'.

> "No 1 has a Greek Doric porch and harpoons and other images of whaling carved on the friezes and the capitals of the pilasters."

The harpoon-shaped iron railings of the two earlier houses show the past connections with the whaling industry, which ceased around 1838. Wood's map of 1822 shows the owner of No 1 as M Dickson Esq; John M Dickson was manager of the Berwick Whale Fishing Company.

On his 'perambulations', Pevsner commented: "No 1 has a Greek Doric porch and harpoons and other images of whaling carved on the friezes and the capitals of the pilasters".[40] At the rear is a

2 & 3 WELLINGTON TERRACE

round-headed window with Gothic lancet design. No 2 has a door surround of two Tuscan pillars with plain capitals. No 3 has unusual (for Berwick) horizontal window panes, a Scottish influence (also to be seen at No 21 Quay Walls). This house was built mid-nineteenth century but in a style in harmony with Nos 1 & 2. The porch has two Tuscan pillars, with Ionic capitals.

12 THE MAIN GUARD

> " ... swords and bayonets were seen glancing among the crowd in great numbers, the most dreadful oaths and groans were heard in every quarter. "

In the days when soldiers guarded the town, the 'Main Guard' or 'Town Guard' building was in Marygate, on various sites over the years. The Guard was needed: they turned out in June 1804 to help quell a riot between a recruiting party of the 'York reserve' and the inhabitants; 'upwards of a thousand people were on the streets, and swords and bayonets were seen glancing among the crowd in great numbers, the most dreadful oaths and groans were heard in every quarter'. Quietness was soon restored with the help of the Main Guard and the Mayor and officers.[71]

The Main Guard was moved to the present Palace Street location early in the nineteenth century, probably around 1815-1816. It was thought that the original building was rebuilt here, but as it is architecturally quite different from the Marygate building as illustrated in Fuller's *History* of 1799, it is more likely that this building was new at the time. The Tuscan pillars are quite worn, but the building has been there in an exposed position near the river for two hundred years.

In 1971, when the building was listed, it was disused and the windows boarded up. Since 1993, however, it has had, and has, more peaceful, non-military uses: the building, which has three rooms inside, including

THE MAIN GUARD FROM THE WALLS

what was the lock-up, is open to the public as a museum in the summer months; and in 1993 it formed the backdrop for a production of *The Merry Wives of Windsor*.

The walls are of coursed, rough sandstone, the front portico having four Tuscan pillars with a huge pediment; the windows were originally rounded. It looks like an Etruscan temple, being both an interesting contrast and a link with the surrounding Georgian housing.

13 QUAY WALLS NOS 19-23

QUAY WALLS NOS 19-22, WITH INSET FOR NO 21

Quay Walls numbers 1 - 23 and Bridge Terrace form Berwick's iconic Georgian riverside panorama. The "striking views of the Quay Walls and Quayside together create one of the definitive pictures of the town, and one of the most distinctive pictures of any town in the region".[30] Pevsner describes it as "A splendid street of well-restored and maintained Georgian houses built immediately behind the riverside town walls, indeed with the wall-head forming the pavement outside the houses. None of the houses is a disappointment".[40] "All the listed buildings in Quay Walls form a Grade II group in view of their prominence as the river frontage of Berwick".[36]

No 23 has a quaint wonky open pediment over the doorway, with Tuscan pilasters either side, and a plain, oblong fanlight. The corners of the building have rusticated quoins, and the internal window shutters have been retained.

The positioning of the windows, doorway and dormers of No. 22 show a wonderful symmetry, all under a pantiled roof. It has an open pediment over the doorway and elaborate scrolling at the side.

No 21 is the former home of Berwick artist Thomas Sword Good, and now used for holiday self-catering accommodation. It has two Venetian-style windows on each floor, and on the ground and first floors horizontal window panes, similar to No 3 Wellington Terrace. In contrast to the stone facades of Nos 23 & 22, this building is rendered and brightly painted.

Thomas Sword Good was born in Berwick on 2 December 1789. He trained initially as a house painter, but from his mid-twenties for about 20 years he exhibited widely - at the Edinburgh Exhibition Society, the British Institution, the Suffolk Street gallery of the Society of British Artists and the Royal Academy; he also exhibited at various regional centres, including Glasgow, Carlisle, Liverpool, Newcastle, Exeter, and Bristol. One of his works was a painting in oils of 'Jimmy Strength'

QUAY WALLS NOS 19-23

(see Section 8). Due to illness he painted little after about 1833. He died at 21 Quay Walls 15 April 1872 and was buried on 19 April in Berwick parish churchyard.[28]

No 20 is tall and thin, with three storeys above pavement level, and a side entrance; it is decorated across the front with a narrow fret of interlaced arches.

The stone surface of No 19 is scoured, as though from a receding ice sheet; or, as Charles Hanson of *Bargain Hunt* fame might say of an antique: "It bears the scars of history"! Some of the stone on the facade was renewed in 2016.

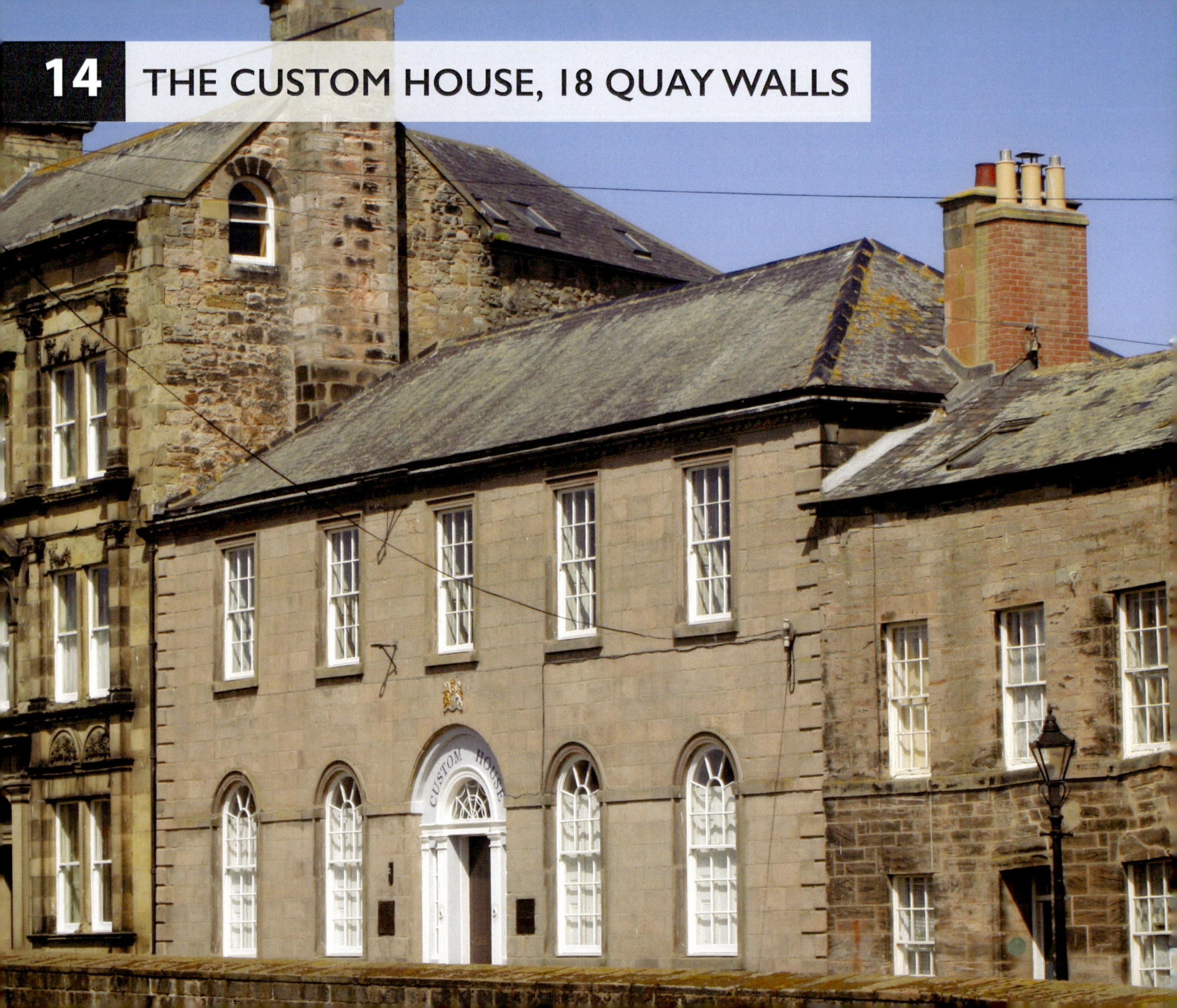

14 THE CUSTOM HOUSE, 18 QUAY WALLS

> *"The building ... boasts an impressive Venetian doorway, with fluted pilasters and a fanlight of intricate tracery."*

No 18 Quay Walls is the old Custom House, an eighteenth century Grade 1 listed building, still with the Coat of Arms above the doorway. It has had many uses in its time: built originally as a private house, it is shown as a 'General Bank' on Wood's map in 1822; it was a Dispensary from 1826 to 1874 when the new Infirmary was opened; a Soldiers' Home around 1914, and finally a Custom House from about 1922 until about 1957, when it reverted to being a private residence. New owners purchased the house in 2016.

The Custom House was not always at this address; it existed from at least 1785.[71] Towards the end of the eighteenth century, when it was probably located at 2 Quay Walls, Fuller lists 31 staff altogether, including six Tide Waiters, two Land Waiters and twelve Coast Waiters.[45] By 1852 the Custom House had moved further along Quay Walls to No 13, where it was located until at least 1902.

The building has a very symmetrical facade, and boasts an impressive Venetian doorway, with fluted pilasters and a fanlight of intricate tracery with what looks like a maritime design. It has a former ice-house underneath, and at the rear there is still a parking sign for Customs & Excise.

THE CUSTOM HOUSE, 18 QUAY WALLS AND (INSET) COAT OF ARMS ABOVE DOORWAY

15 THE CHANDLERY, AND QUAY WALLS NOS 15-17

QUAY WALLS NOS 16 & 17

The Chandlery, restored and converted, currently comprises the 'Lowry's at the Chandlery' cafe, opened July 2014, and several offices. A building on the site in the 1850's showed a smithy and stores. It was restored in 1987-1988 after being purchased by English Estates North from the Berwick Harbour Commission.

QUAY WALLS NO 15

Nos 16 & 17 Quay Walls are partly late eighteenth century but mostly around 1870. Classical door surround with Doric pilasters, and pediment; the ground floor windows have carved foliage above. The houses were restored in 2016.

No 15 Quay Walls, Gate House (because of its location adjacent to Shore Gate), is the higher level above 19 & 21 Sandgate, with small, twelve-paned sash windows, and two dormers. The property is currently (December 2016) for sale.

On the Quayside, the mid-nineteenth century Victorian brick building is now a photographers'; the site in 1852 was a saw pit. The building dates from the second half of the nineteenth century as it is shown on the 1897 map. Facing the river, the old building to the left of the car park is listed as a 'Store' in the Shipbuilders Yard in mid-nineteenth century; it is now abandoned and overgrown.

Berwick boasted its own shipbuilding industry from the middle of the eighteenth century until 1878; it was then revived in 1950 for almost thirty years. Cranes and partly built boats towered over the surrounding buildings - there are many photographs in the illustrated books on Berwick showing the busy Quay, and a good source for the history of the industry can be found on www.berwickshipyard.com.[65] The last ship to be launched was a schooner, *Audela*, in April 1979; it now has a restaurant in Bridge Street named after it.

16 SANDGATE

SANDGATE, EAST SIDE, FROM SHORE GATE

Sandgate (earlier names Segate, Shoregate) was an integral part of the medieval layout of the town's roads, and shown in the *True Description* map of the town around 1580. In the Rawlinson health report of 1850, Sandgate was "frequently flooded at the lower end; the houses are consequently damp. The sewage and flood water is at times two or three feet deep. The economy of proper sewers and drains would be very great, not only here but throughout the whole town."[50]

Shore Gate is a Grade I listed structure. A gateway is shown here on the *True Description* map of around 1580; in surveys of 1596 & 1597: "The shore gate next the river, where the ships arrive—the lower part is in great decay"......"The Masendue (or Keyside) and Shoare gates.—These need repair only, which with the stuff and workmanship will cost by estimation 25l."[11] The present construction is thought to date from 1760, and still retains its original timber doors.

Looking up Sandgate, on the right, between the Walls and Silver Street, there were five public houses in the mid-nineteenth century: *The London & Berwick Tavern*, *The Hen & Chickens Hotel*, *The Golden Swan Inn*, *The Fishers Arms Inn*, and *The Peacock Inn*.[6] Today, however, only *The Hen & Chickens Hotel* remains and is unoccupied; it was built in the eighteenth century. Pevsner, writing when *The Hen & Chickens* was still flourishing, commented: "11-15 is a good mid 18th century group, typical of Berwick with their bright paintwork, moulded window surrounds, scrolled kneelers and steeply pitched roofs".[40] A Berwick-upon-Tweed Council publication of 1995 said of the hotel that is was a "long constituted rallying ground of principal grain merchants, cattle dealers and other business men frequenting the Berwick markets".[29] In 1806 the Union Coach from Newcastle to Edinburgh stopped in Berwick, the stop shared by several coaching inns, including the *Hen and Chickens*, and the *King's Arms* on Hide Hill.

Nos 11 and 13 Sandgate, currently used as offices, are eighteenth

SANDGATE, WEST SIDE, FROM SHORE GATE

century, with open pediments over the doorways, pantiled roofs and tall brick chimney stacks.

> "... a granary in the nineteenth century; this was demolished to make way for a cinema in 1914... an 'austere, pedimented, brick shed', with noisy seats."

Beyond is the old Corn Exchange, of a mixed renaissance style, currently occupied as offices and apartments in 22 units. It was opened as a Corn Exchange on 28 June 1858, but sometimes acted as a theatre by hosting plays. When it ceased to operate as a Corn Exchange, it housed the town's swimming pool from the early 1970s until 1998. The Friends of Berwick and District Museum and Archives website has much information on this building.[18]

Beyond Sandgate, on Hide Hill (earlier Uddinggate), is the *King's Arms Hotel*, "…designed just like a typical Georgian country house".[40] In the early nineteenth century, the mail coach always stopped at the *King's Arms*, as did the Union Coach for three months of the year. A theatre was established, behind the hotel, by Stephen Kemble, manager of the Theatre Royal in Edinburgh; it opened on Monday 11th August 1794, with the comic opera *Lionel and Clarissa*. The hotel has many associations with Charles Dickens and is still used as a hotel and restaurant.

Further up the hill, and currently a restaurant and shops, is the Berwick Theatre; it opened with the film *The Flag Lieutenant* on 2nd February 1928. It has a classical facade, designed by Southport architect Albert Schofield.[39]

Looking up Sandgate, on the left, there were three public houses in the mid-nineteenth century, to add to the five on the right: *The Ship Tavern Public House*, *The Old Nags Head Inn*, and *The Nags Head Inn*. On the corner with Driver's Lane there was a granary in the nineteenth century; this was demolished to make way for a cinema in 1914 - Pictureland (Berwick) Ltd opened the Playhouse cinema on the site in June 1914, an 'austere, pedimented, brick shed', with noisy seats.[49] Excavations on the site after the Playhouse was demolished showed deposits that "comprise the walls and surfaces of buildings, and associated debris and demolition material. These features may relate to the 19th century granary building and/or earlier buildings which occupied the site".[3] There are current plans for a 60-bed Premier Inn hotel on the site; detailed plans and illustrations can be seen on the Northumberland County Council website.

No 10 is an eighteenth century listed building, now offices, with three storeys with rusticated quoins. No 8 is not listed but thought to be eighteenth century.

The Queens Head Hotel (Nos 4 & 6) is early nineteenth century and comprises the former *Old Nag's Head Inn* and the *Nag's Head Inn*; it is still in business. *The Old Nag's Head Inn* changed its name to *The Queen's Head* and later (sometime between 1914 and 1925) amalgamated with *The Nag's Head Inn* under the name *The Queen's Head*.

QUAY WALLS NOS 10-14 | 17

QUAY WALLS NOS 10-13

QUAY WALLS NOS 10-13

QUAY WALLS NO 14

There is never a dull moment on Quay Walls, with the general hub-bub echoing around, from the trains crossing the river and running along the scenic route through Tweedmouth and Spittal, the traffic on the old bridge and its newer neighbour, the oars-men and women battling with the tidal river, and the many visitors attracted by the interesting facets of the Berwick waterfront.

No 14 Quay Walls is the upper part of the building No 5 on Driver's Lane. Nos 10-13 Quay Walls were known as 'Quayside Buildings'.

Nos 10-11 have the same roof line, so were probably built at the same time. No 12 is higher, and No 13 lower than 10-12. Nos 12 & 13 were restored by Berwick Preservation Trust: "These Quay Wall properties were built in 1825 and leased to H M Customs who used them as a custom house for the Port of Berwick. In 1917, they became private houses but by 1971 they were empty, boarded up and falling down".[31] Work commenced 15 January 1973, requiring "a complete internal gut & rebuilding" and roof retiled using pantiles.[7] No 11 is currently (December 2016) for sale for £275,000.

QUAY WALLS NOS 8-9, BRIDGE STREET   18

QUAY WALLS NOS 8 & 9

A PEEP TOWARDS BRIDGE STREET

Nos 8 & 9 Quay Walls are eighteenth century houses, the former currently 'The Walls' guest house. Nos 8 and 8A have a pair of doors under shared pediment: "two adjoining doorways tied together by one big and awkward pediment"[40]. Around 1914, it was the Queen Victoria Nurses' Home. No 9, with its brightly painted rendering and prominent porch and windows, has a large timber hoist housing incorporated into the living area at the rear.

A peep into the rear of Bridge Street (was Briggate) shows Wilson's Cycles - now (May 2017) Berwick Cycles - and the entrance to the car park which replaced *The Old Bridge Tavern* (formerly the *Old Hen & Chickens Inn*). The building was demolished in June 1963 to give access to the public car park behind Bridge Street; a late 16th-century wallpainting uncovered in the building was removed and conserved, and is now in storage at Berwick Museum in the Barracks. The Berwick Civic Society's Buildings Study Group has produced studies on the buildings on the north and south sides of Bridge Street.[32]

19 BERWICK YHA, DEWAR'S LANE

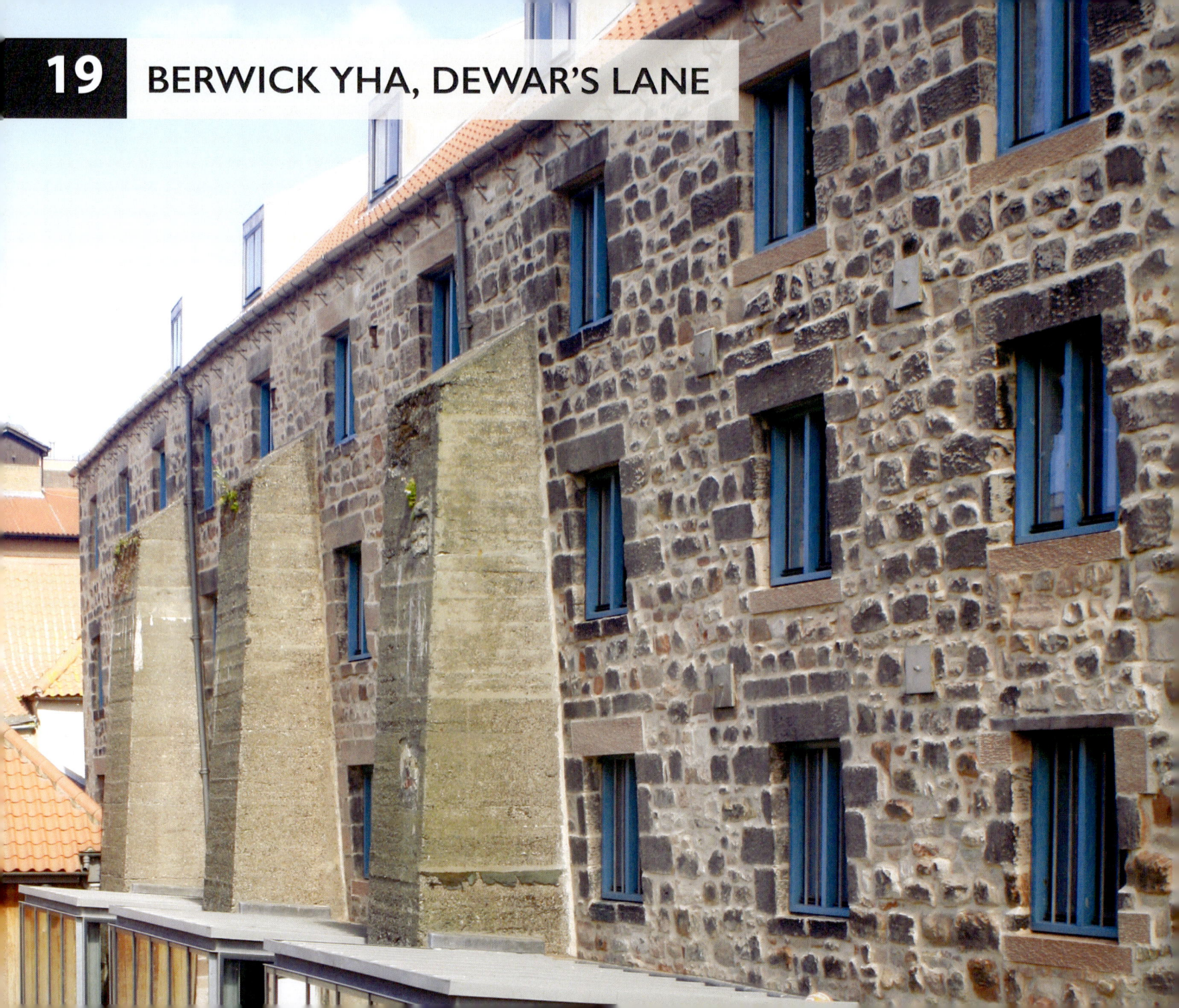

From the walls you see the other side of the leaning former granary made famous by Lowry; the massive buttresses are reassuring! The building, restored by Berwick Preservation Trust, opened its doors on 18 February 2011 as a 55-bed Youth Hostels Association hostel, with an exhibition centre, conference facilities and bistro open to the public. The inaugural exhibition showed photographs by Mark Irving.

> "A tunnel was cut through the town wall south of the granary in the nineteenth century ..."

The Granary was built in the mid- to late-eighteenth century and has been altered in subsequent centuries. A tunnel was cut through the town wall south of the granary in the nineteenth century and a tramway provided a direct link to the harbour; the rails can still be seen. The building was used by a firm of seed and grain merchants until 1985.

Plans were put forward in 1991 to demolish the building, but were later withdrawn; it was February 2006 when new plans were drawn up for the Youth Hostel and other uses. An archaeological dig on the site in 2004 had revealed twelfth- to fifteenth-century pottery, and cobbled and flagstone surfaces.[5] The renovated building was opened 'officially' on 3 June 2011 by The Lord Lieutenant of Northumberland, The Duchess of Northumberland.

BERWICK YHA, FORMER GRANARY IN DEWAR'S LANE

20 QUAY WALLS NOS 6-7, QUAYSIDE LOOK-OUT

ANOTHER PEEP TOWARDS BRIDGE STREET

THE QUAYSIDE LOOKOUT

The steps down lead to Sally Port and Bridge Street, the building on far right on Bridge Street - since 1982 The Magna Tandoori Restaurant - was The Old Hen and Chickens public house.

The Quayside Lookout, a former nineteenth century public convenience, redundant for about 30 years, was acquired by the Berwick Preservation Trust in 1997 and converted into office accommodation. It was recently privately owned and open to the public as a craft workshop, but was sold by auction in October 2016.

Nos 6 & 7 Quay Walls are early nineteenth century, No 7 being William Weatherhead's solicitors in 1914. Nos 6 & 7 form a group, with pantiles on the roofs and brick chimneys, with No 7 noticeably wider than No 6.

21 QUAY WALLS NOS 3-5

QUAY WALLS NO 3

QUAY WALLS NOS 4 & 5

Nos 4 & 5 Quay Walls are eighteenth century. No 5, dating back to 1770, was donated to the Berwick Preservation Trust around 1972. It was restored by the Trust and renamed Collingwood House after the donor, the late Lt Col Collingwood. It is currently (December 2016) for sale at £375,000. No 4 is now used as offices; "No 4, late 18th is five bays with a pedimented Tuscan door surround and an especially ornate Venetian inner doorway".[40]

No 3 Quay Walls is a former eighteenth-century granary and possibly the earliest surviving granary in the town. The building was leased by the Salvation Army as their Barracks from 1884 to 1957. Its first meeting was in August 1884, when the Major Dowdle gave an address on the 'Good Samaritan'. The new Citadel opened in Church Street in late 1956, so by the following year "The Registrar General, being satisfied that the undermentioned buildings have wholly ceased to be used as places of worship by the congregations on whose behalf they were certified in accordance with the Places of Worship Registration Act, 1955, has cancelled the record of their certifications: Salvation Army Hall, Quay Walls, Berwick. Date of Certification: 8th October, 1884".[19] The building was acquired and restored by the Berwick Preservation Trust and converted into nine flats, and offices; the work was completed in 1988. Eight small windows across were retained in the restoration; the dormers were not present immediately prior to restoration.

QUAY WALLS NO 3

22 QUAY WALLS NOS 1-2

QUAY WALLS NO 1

QUAY WALLS NO 2

No 2 Quay Walls is quite different from those preceding, being one storey facing the river; it's probably early nineteenth century - around that time the Custom House was located at No 2 Quay Walls (see Section 14). The house is rendered and painted, under a slate roof.

No 1 is even more recent, being in the Gothic revival style and built in 1869. Its site has much history: the crow stepped gables are a feature imitating the same on the medieval buildings it replaced. Those medieval buildings replaced a hospital, the Maison Dieu, founded by Philip de Rydale in the thirteenth century. In 1888 Scott wrote that "this house was undoubtedly situated at the corner of the present bridge, where the National Bank now stands".[51] There used to be a 'Quay Gate' at the end of the walls near the cobbled slope leading down to the Quay, as well as the 'English Gate' (or 'Bridge Gate') at the north end of the seventeenth century bridge; both these gates were still in place in 1822, but removed shortly afterwards.

QUAY WALLS NO 2

23 BERWICK BRIDGE

Berwick Bridge is one of the finest seventeenth century road bridges in the country and is still used by traffic, although only one-way - after trials it was decided to opt for a north-to-south one-way system. It was built between 1611 and 1634, but was probably in use from about 1624. Fuller describes its construction in great detail, including what the workmen were paid.[45] As it was one of the few entrances to the town, the bridge was fortified at the north end by a guarded gate (the 'English Gate', sometimes called the 'Bridge Gate').

There have been at least four timber bridges documented, with the latest one being shown, a little to the north of the present bridge, on the *True Description* map of about 1580. The idea of a stone bridge was being mentioned from at least 1564.

On 25 May 1607, the existing timber bridge was damaged and became impassable. An estimate of £5440 10s 4d for a stone bridge was put forward; this was a design of six arches by James Burrell. An unsigned document of June 1607 stated that "…there is an old [medieval] foundation of a stone bridge, about 40 yards from the timber bridge towards the sea, which if it be good, as by likelihood it is, a great part of the charge will be eased".[28] In April 1611 a new estimate was arrived at of £8462 8s 4d, signed by James Burrell as 'Bridge Maister'. By a warrant from the Crown dated 16 May 1611, money was made available, but the cost was not to exceed £8000.[67]

As part of the agreement, timber was to be used from the royal forest of Chopwell, which is now Chopwell Woodland Park, near Gateshead; the Park is open to the public, with miles of paths for walking and cycling. There are still remnants of the ancient forest on the more inaccessible crags above the river Derwent.[57]

Work started on the bridge on 19 June 1611, with the workforce including 31 masons, 2 slaters, 9 smiths, 22 quarrymen and wallers, 76 labourers and 9 boys. Stone was carried by water from a quarry at Tweedmouth. Construction proceeded without incident, but the £8000 had been used up by May 1617, when they estimated another £4000 or £5000 was required; the extra money was granted - for the bridge and a church.

A report of 1620 gives progress as generally favourable - construction work was 'workmanlike and substanciallie well wrought'.[67] The Bishop of Durham became involved, being asked on 17 July 1620 to take the finishing of the bridge under his special care. By August 1620 seven of the 14 arches now proposed, starting from the north end, had been completed; the eighth was in preparation. The 'landstall' on the south side was also in progress, with first arch and pier adjoining. The bishop thought work was going too slowly, and King James I agreed; he expected that, with the bishop's care, the work would be finished 'in all pointes fitt for soe Royall a Monument of blessed union between the two kingdomes'.[67] By a contract dated 12 October 1620, the aim was for the bridge to be fit for traffic by midsummer 1621, and walls and paving by 1622. Work proceeded more speedily, with all the arches completed by Michaelmas 1621.

However, in October that year disaster struck; the Tweed flooded as never in living memory. Floating haystacks and loose timber bore down on the old wooden bridge, part of which broke away and crashed against the new bridge. A whole year's work was undone in a few hours, several arches near the south end being destroyed. Work restarted 8 April 1622. Accounts were not closed until 24 October 1634, the total cost being £12,522 1s 9d, plus a few other payments, bringing the grand total to £14,960 1s 6d. Total exchequer grants amounted to £15000, leaving only £39 18s 6d for a church!

In 1622, wages were being paid to masons, smiths, lightermen, quarrymen and labourers, as well as the Surveyor, James Burrell. By 1623-24 women were also being employed for 'sanding' the new bridge, which suggests the bridge was nearing completion. From 1624 onwards the

MODERN BOATS TIED UP AT THE QUAY

number employed was greatly reduced, the main employees being two lightermen and a few labourers; masons were still employed at the quarry on and off between 1626 and 1627. In October 1624 the men were employed in dismantling the old timber bridge, so presumably the new stone bridge was passable for traffic by this time.[7]

In the 1720s, Daniel Defoe wrote: "visited that old frontier, where indeed there is one thing very fine, and that is, the bridge over the Tweed, …, a noble, stately work, consisting of sixteen arches, and joining, as may be said, the two kingdoms."[13] In 1850, Rawlinson, with the Royal Border Bridge just completed, was less than complimentary when he wrote that "compared with the new and majestic railway viaduct it is insignificant".[50] Pevsner wrote: "A beautiful red sandstone bridge of 15 segmental arches with Doric columns on many of the cutwaters".[40] The Doric columns can still be seen on the taller cutwaters towards the north end of the bridge. 14, 15 or 16 arches? An advantage of the bridge surviving is that we can still count them - actually 15, with those nearer the north end higher where the river flows deeper.

Before the start of construction of the Royal Tweed Bridge in 1923 the *Berwickshire News & General Advertiser* wrote about the stone bridge: "Those sturdy, thick set limbs, sunk far below the bed of the river, give one the impression that they can bear the intense strain for another 286 years, and still look the future in the face as only such a structure can, i.e. without fear or trembling. Those 15 arches stand today like the Sphinx or the Pyramids amidst the sands of the great silent Egyptian desert, relics of the lost art in structural stone masonry, and a direct challenge to the age of steel".[71]

At the beginning of the twentieth century, with the advent of motorised vehicles and increased volume of traffic it became increasingly clear that the old bridge was not suitable for the 'class and quantity of present day traffic',[71] and various answers to the problems were offered, including widening the bridge, driving a tunnel under the Tweed, and building a completely new bridge. One petition from some leading artists and architects spoke of the bridge's 'picturesque position and extreme beauty from every point of view', regarding it as part of our national inheritance and urged the town 'to allow it to remain intact'.[7]

It was finally decided to construct a new bridge. When the Royal Tweed Bridge was completed in 1928, the intention was that the old bridge would be used for foot passengers only. Today, 88 years later, there is still talk of removing vehicles from the old bridge - maybe it can become Berwick's answer to the 'Pont des Arts'?

BRIDGE END 24

WEST STREET IN AUGUST 2015

Bridge End was one of the busiest areas of Berwick for many centuries, as it was one of the few entrances to the town via the present stone bridge and the earlier timber bridges; and until the Royal Tweed Bridge opened in 1928, it was the main A1 route between England and Scotland. For many centuries Bridge Street (Briggate) was the main street for shopping and trade.

In medieval times there were at least three friaries and/or hospitals at this end of Bridge Street, as well as houses, granaries, shops and pubs. Human burials, from as early as the thirteenth century, have been uncovered by archaeological investigations in the Love Lane area; and a wall uncovered that may have been part of one of the religious houses.

The House of the Friars of the Sack at Berwick didn't survive very long and was taken over by the Dominicans - the Bishop of St Andrews was instructed to sell the site to the Dominicans. Cowe identifies the site as the Chapel of Ravensdale on the north side of Love Lane, once the extreme western end of Briggate.[3,44] There are fragile documents relating to the Chapell of Ravensdell or Ravensdowne from 1614 and 1647 in the Berwick Archives, so the chapel clearly survived until at least the mid-seventeenth century.[7] A plan of about 1810 by Richard Todd shows the area "formerly known by the names of Ravens, or Ravens Dale, the old Chapel and waste grounds adjoining"; this area corresponds to the present Tintagel House and the spare land adjoining.[7]

Excavations carried out by Tyne and Wear Museums to the south of Love Lane in 1998 revealed medieval structural remains and ten burials. These may be associated with the site of St Edward's Hospital (see below) which was eventually taken into use by the Trinitarian friars. Cowan and Easson say that the Trinitarians had settled in Berwick before 1240-48 and that "they may have established themselves in the hospital of St Edward or Bridge House on their arrival. Although it is only from 1306 that there is evidence of their possessing Bridge House, while certain identification of the house of the Trinitarians with this hospital comes only from 1386".[30,74]

The Maison Dieu hospital was founded by Philip de Rydale during the reign of Alexander III (1249-1286). The Patent Rolls for Edward I in 1300 include "confirmation of a grant…which the king has inspected, by Philip de Rydale to the master, chaplains and poor of the hospital of the Domus Dei of Berwick-on-Tweed…".[30] The hospital stood on the site between the present *Barrels Inn* and No. 1 Quay Walls.

As regards the Hospital of St Edward, the *Patent Rolls* cite Henry III, in August 1246, as having granted 'protection without term, for the master and brethren of the house of St Edward on the bridge of Berwick'.[3] There seems to be some confusion at times between this hospital, sometimes called Domus Pontis, and Domus Dei (see Maison Dieu above).

Nos 2-12 on the west side of Bridge End continue the Georgian theme, being built in the early nineteenth century; all have retained their Georgian windows.

The south end of West Street is shown above in August 2015, a similar view to that painted by Lowry, and later in November 2015 - a year-long restoration of the former William Cowe & Sons buildings on either side of West Street had begun in 2015, and was still ongoing in February 2017.

Lowry visited Berwick regularly from about 1935 until shortly before he died in 1976; his *Painting by Bridge End* dates from around 1939.[27] In 2015, a limited edition (of 650 signed in pencil by artist) of the print Bridge End sold at auction in London for £8,610, ten times its asking price.[70]

WEST STREET IN NOVEMBER 2015

25 BRIDGE TERRACE AND LOVE LANE

Bridge Terrace continues the Georgian theme with buildings facing the river, No 1 being early nineteenth century and part of No 12 Bridge End, with prominent rustication on the ground floor. Nos 2 & 3 (Berwick House) may have been one house originally; they are eighteenth century. "No 2 is brightly painted and has a handsome door case with Tuscan pilasters set in front of a rusticated surround".[40] The door case of No 3 has fluted pilasters. At some stage the windows have been altered, those on the ground floor being plain sashes while those on the first floor are 12-paned.

The building to the left of Nos 2 & 3 is on the site of a former granary at the end of Bridge Terrace and Love Lane (formerly Bank Alley); the granary was demolished in 1978 and replaced by retirement flats, called The Granary, for Anchor Housing Association; the twelve flats were occupied by 1980. This site would have been very close to the end of the medieval timber bridge.

On the north side of Love Lane is Tintagel House, a former granary converted for residential use in 1936/37 (formerly owned by Alexander Darling, of Messrs Johnson & Darlings Ltd, seed and grain merchant), and first occupied soon after October 1937. In the conversion, sections of the outer walls of the granary on the sides and the rear were retained, as were some of the stone supporting pillars inside the building and under the present terrace at the front. The front of the building was rebuilt about 20 feet back from Love Lane; the original building line was directly overlooking the lane. The difference in stone work can be seen between the rough, random-sized stone at the sides, indicative of an industrial building, and the more uniformly laid stonework at the front. A photograph showing the 'Cat Wall' at the rear of the original property is included in *A descriptive account of Berwick-upon-Tweed*.[29] Tintagel House and the adjoining land at the side cover the site of the former Ravensdale Chapel. (See Section 24).

From the end of Love Lane, a 'New Road' was built around 1816

BRIDGE TERRACE

63

TINTAGEL HOUSE AND LOVE LANE

along the river to give employment after the end of the Napoleonic Wars. Johnstone, writing in 1817, wrote: "…two roads from the town, one leading to the new pier, and the other down the steep banks, near the old castle, along the side of the river above a mile, were projected and immediately begun, and upwards of 160 people employed in daily labour, who would otherwise have severely felt the pressure of the times". Johnstone wrote that these roads "were lately finished,…".[47]

ROYAL TWEED BRIDGE 26

ROYAL TWEED BRIDGE

The Royal Tweed Bridge, a road bridge, was begun in 1925 and officially opened by the Prince of Wales, the future Edward VIII, on 16 May 1928. The span of the arches increases towards the northern, deeper, side of the river - the old bridge employed larger arches on the north side too. The view through the northern arch towards the Royal Border Bridge shows a Virgin East Coast train on its way to Kings Cross - Stagecoach Group and Virgin Group were awarded the franchise for the East Coast line in November 2014.

"Designed 1925-1928 by L.G. Mouchel & Partners, the concrete engineers. Spans 428 metres (1,405ft) in four long leaps, with segmental arches, each built up on four ribs. [Lacks elegance] …a pity, as the opportunity in a town like Berwick and within sight of the other two bridges was enormous. Even worse than this lost opportunity was the damage done by the bridge to the integrity of Marygate".[40] "When built, the bridge possessed the longest reinforced concrete arch in Britain and was also the country's longest highway viaduct".[38]

The idea of building a new bridge was conceived at least as far back as 1896. As the volume of traffic increased with the advent of motorised vehicles, the old bridge could not cope, particularly when stubborn drivers confronted each other, as in August 1923: "One of our motor buses met a large char-a-banc. It was seen in a moment that they could not pass each other….which of the two had to retreat? Neither driver felt inclined to do so, both contending they had the first claim to proceed forward. A rather stormy altercation took place, during which time traffic was being held up, and passengers were getting uneasy. As the situation became more and more threatening, the driver of the char-a-banc very reluctantly went back, our local man following up with the smile of triumph on his hitherto perturbed face".[71]

From an indenture of 1 May 1924, between Northumberland County Council and Mayor etc of Berwick, the "….existing bridge is of insufficient width and otherwise ill-adapted to meet the requirements of the public…". 75% of the price of the new bridge would be paid for by the Ministry of Transport.[7] The contract for construction of the bridge was agreed with Holloway Bros Ltd in November 1924, with work well under way by March 1925. The annual bridge-to-bridge swimming race took place August 1925, avoiding the new obstacles that had appeared since the previous year; this race was instituted in 1912, with a challenge cup presented by Lord Grey, and was held annually until at least the late 1950s.

Photographs appeared in the newspapers at various times over the next three years; by December 1925 good progress had been made, with some of the concrete ribs of the first span in place. There were casualties: in March 1926 a William Pennock, from West Hartlepool, fell about 30 feet onto the river bed while the tide was out, injuring his legs, and was taken to Berwick Infirmary. It was later found that his injuries were not so severe as first thought - a bruised hip and ankle. Presumably he soon returned to work!

There were several discoveries made during construction, including pre-historic red deer's antlers; a coal seam (the thickest layer being about 8 inches) on the northern bank, said to be an outcrop of one of the Scremerston seams; and the piles of the timber bridge which preceded the stone bridge.[71] The line of this timber bridge starts from between Love Lane and the foot of Bank Hill, some 50 or 60 yards up river from the stone bridge.

The new bridge was tested by a severe flood in September 1926 and, unlike the old bridge in October 1621, it survived; very high floods brought timber and rubbish down the river, but the piling stood firm.

For Christmas 1926 Messrs Martin's Printing Works issued a Christmas postcard, with a view of Berwick's three bridges; it claimed to give a 'splendid' idea of what the Tweed valley would look like when the new bridge was completed - and just 2d each! Martins The Printers, established in 1892, is still in business to this day (in fact, are responsible for printing this book!)

By July 1927 it was possible to walk the whole way across the river on the new structure, but only by taking your life in your hands, as members of the Institute of Transport found: "It is now possible to walk or climb right across the river on the structure without using the gangway, and some of the members walked along the decking, across a portion not yet completed via two planks, to another part of the decking, and along the woodwork which will eventually receive the crown of the largest span…"[70]. It was hoped to open the bridge for foot passengers when safe after December 1927, but this did not happen until the official opening in May 1928.

For the official opening, the Prince of Wales travelled by overnight sleeper train from King's Cross, opened the bridge, saying in his speech that erecting bridges over the Tweed river seemed to have been a habit in these parts, and left on the 2.38pm train back to London. The road from the southern end of new bridge to the old A1 was named 'Prince Edward Road'.[71]

What about the old bridge? In January 1927 the intention was to use it for foot passengers only, as it was not suitable for the fast moving traffic of that day. 89 years later…!

27 ICE HOUSE, LEAPING SALMON

The CORPORATIONS
ICADEMY. 1798.

ICE HOUSE ON BANK HILL (COURTESY OF BERWICK PRESERVATION TRUST)

The Ice House was built towards the end of the eighteenth century to store ice used in the salmon trade; it was one of several ice houses in the town. Ice houses were not shown on maps until 1852. In Good's Directory of 1806 it was written of salmon: "it is all sent to London, in boxes, with ice, by a company of coopers, most of which are ship-owners….The number of boxes of salmon shipped every season to London is from 10,000 to 12,000".[46]

The entrance tunnel to the ice house has a barrel vaulted roof; this leads to the main chamber which, although reduced from the original size, is vast. In a report in 1811 it was discovered that by striking against the inner door, the sound heightens and increases until its reverberations imitate the rolling of thunder…"[71] The ice house is cared for by Berwick Preservation Trust: "Bank Hill Ice House was one of several built in Berwick in the early eighteenth century. The ice was sourced locally if the winter had been severe enough, but usually was imported from Norway. The blocks were carefully stored in layers with sawdust laid between the blocks to prevent them from freezing into a solid mass. Without this facility, much of eighteenth century Berwick's wealth may not have been created. The ice was used for packing fish, particularly salmon, in crates to be transported to London. Ice houses were still being used in the 1930s, and Bank Hill was designated an air raid shelter during the Second World War".[31]

The Leaping Salmon pub was built at the end of the eighteenth century as a Corporation Academy for children of freemen, bringing together former schools including the writing and reading schools which were at that time reported to be unhealthy - the children "are obtaining their education at the expense of their health"[8]. Plans were drawn up in June 1798, and by early December that year the building was ready for its slate roof. It was probably occupied by the children some time in 1799.

Fuller, a doctor of medicine and so concerned for the health of the children, wrote in 1799: "The Corporation has built a large and elegant school-house. It consists of five spacious rooms, with suitable offices, which are to be appropriated for the mathematical school, the writing, and the three reading schools. It is most delightfully situated on the Bank-hill adjoining to the grammar school. Four of the rooms fully face the Tweed, and command a complete view of the bridge. The situation is dry, and it enjoys a very free ventilation, which must contribute highly to the health of the scholars".[45] The building has rusticated quoins and surviving 24-pane windows. Further along Golden Square is the former Grammar School, now a Baptist Church, built in 1820. The Corporation Academy building still functioned as a school when the hall next door was built around 1906.

On the left-hand side of the path, opposite *The Leaping Salmon*, there are steps down to the river where the listed boathouse belonging to the Berwick Amateur Rowing Club is located. The Club, and the boathouse, date back to 1869; the boathouse was later extended. When listed in 2010, it was described as "an attractive and largely intact club boathouse displaying the characteristic features of boat store, club house, balcony and viewing tower".[38]

28 BANK HILL

BANK HILL UNITED PRESBYTERIAN CHURCH

BANK HILL UNITED PRESBYTERIAN CHURCH

ROYAL TWEED BRIDGE AND TWEEDMOUTH

The main part of the United Presbyterian Church (Zion Chapel) was built between 1835 and 1837 - by a lease of 14 May 1835 the chapel had to be erected and finished within two years.[7] The congregation decreased in numbers later and the chapel was sold to the Congregation of Protestant Dissenters in 1852, with a lease for 283 years![7] On the map of 1852 there is a small vestry attached (shorter and narrower than the extension we now see) at the south end. In 1906 a hall and vestry was added, replacing the original vestry. This hall extension is now a self-catering holiday cottage. The chapel has rusticated base and quoins and four round-headed windows with lancet decoration and Tuscan pilastered doorway.

Lady Jerningham, of Longridge Towers, died on 9th October 1902. Pevsner wrote describing her monument: 'Lady Jerningham Monument, designed by her husband, Sir Hubert Jerningham, with the assistance of Walter Ingram, and carved by Penachini [Pennacchini] in 1906'.[40,69] It was erected in Berwick in 1908 on a spot where at certain times of year it could just about be seen from the Jerningham's home, Longridge Towers.

Lady Jerningham's second husband, the diplomat Sir Hubert Jerningham, was MP for Berwick from 1881-1885. Later he was posted to Trinidad and Tobago, where his wife's health suffered; she returned to Britain but never fully recovered her health.[69] Her death was marked locally: after the funeral, "on the way to the cemetery great crowds lined the streets, shops were respectfully closed, and every blind was drawn".[71] At the unveiling of the statue the Mayor of Berwick spoke of Lady Jerningham's philanthropy: "Generous and kindly she ever was. Her philanthropy reached the humblest. Many had reason to bless her name. For all her goodness we rejoice to know that she is now enjoying her Master's reward".[71] Both Sir Hubert and Lady Jerningham

BANK HILL: LADY JERNINGHAM'S MONUMENT

ROSEMOUNT, BANK HILL

BANK HILL NOS 3-6

are buried in a vault at the rear of Our Lady & St Cuthbert's Church, Ravensdowne. Further up Bank Hill is a row of houses, Nos 3-6, none of which is listed. No 4 is early nineteenth century prior to 1822, and No 6 later in the first half of the nineteenth century, with windows altered to plain sashes. No 3 is newly stone-clad in a development of energy-saving eco homes along with the buildings behind (now called Rosemount). No 5 is probably twentieth century. The name of the road was traditionally Bank Hill; today it seems to be interchangeable between Bankhill (street sign, electoral register) and Bank Hill (Ordnance Survey). In 1822 it was Moors Bank.

MEG'S MOUNT VIEWS AND THE ROYAL BORDER BRIDGE

29

TWEEDMOUTH, ROYAL BORDER BRIDGE AND (INSET) FLYING SCOTSMAN, 14 MAY 2016

WEST END OF TWEEDMOUTH

Meg's Mount (in 1596 called "Roaring Meges mounte") gives almost 360° views which include the Royal Border Bridge, Tweedmouth - with the large, crenellated former Presbyterian Church built in 1848 (more recently it was the Kingdom Hall of the Jehovah's Witnesses and now The Watchtower Gallery - a private art gallery), the Royal Tweed Bridge, the Jacobean bridge, the rooftops of Berwick towards the sea and Holy Island and a former ladies public convenience now converted to selling ice creams! There were plans in 1837 to site the new gaol on Meg's Mount and the adjoining field along Castlegate, but the gaol was eventually built in Wallace Green (see Section 37); at

ROYAL BORDER BRIDGE BY NIGHT

that time the area of Meg's Mount was given as 3 roods, 6 poles and 9 yards!(7)

Of the Royal Border Bridge Pevsner wrote: "Royal Border Bridge. 1847-1850 by Robert Stephenson. 28 arches, each of 18.75 metres (61.5ft) span, and they tower high up like those of a Roman aqueduct. The piers are of rock-faced stone, the round arches of brick, stone-faced. Height 385 metres (126.25 ft)". The foundation stone laid 22 May 1847, without ceremony.(40)

Earlier, in November 1846, a contract was agreed with Messrs McKay and Blackstock for £180,000 for constructing the bridge for the Newcastle and Berwick Railway. By May 1847 work was in progress constructing a temporary wooden bridge, and by December of that year several piers from the south side had been erected 20-30 feet and it was hoped the wooden structure would be completed in the following twelve months. In March 1848 the masons went on strike, asking for a rise in wages from 21s to 24s. In September of that year a test was carried out with a (Third Class) railway carriage back and forth across the wooden bridge, "to the delight and wonder of onlookers", and the next month the temporary timber bridge was open for traffic, thus enabling trains to run from London to Edinburgh and Glasgow without interruption.(71)

THE LOOVRE, FORMER LADIES' PUBLIC CONVENIENCE

By December 1849 all the piers of the stone bridge were in place, with the connecting arches complete within the following two months. Building a bridge in such an environment is testing, especially in winter, and at the end of January 1850 a large amount of ice floated down river and descended on the timber bridge, but it survived intact. A couple of weeks later the last keystone was in place and all the workers were treated to a meal at the King's Arms. By July the stone bridge was sufficiently complete for trains to run over one line of the bridge, which was opened by Queen Victoria and Prince Albert on 29 August 1850. The Queen wrote in her diary: "We passed Mor-

ROOFTOPS OF BERWICK TOWARDS THE SEA AND HOLY ISLAND

peth, Werkworth, & saw Werkworth Castle in the distance. The railroad goes close along the sea, which was beautifully blue. Holy Island (Lindisfarn) was plainly to be seen. We stopped at Alnwick station, & a little after 3, reached Berwick, where we got out & inaugurated the beautiful new bridge, similar to the one at New Castle. Thousands of spectators were assembled & Addresses were presented by the Mayor. Ld Grey took leave us here. — We stopped next at Dunbar, where another Address was presented, & at 5 we arrived at Edinburgh".[71,25]

One very important downside to the location of this bridge was the destruction of much of the remains of the castle to make way for the line and the station. A special highlight of 14 May 2016 was seeing the Flying Scotsman once again crossing the bridge on its way to Edinburgh.

The 'Loovre', a former Ladies' public toilet originally opened in March 1899, is now an ice cream and refreshment kiosk, refurbished by the Berwick Preservation Trust in 2014. Strangely, it doesn't have a loo for the proprietor![7] Reporting in April 1899, John Cruden, income collector for Lavatories, said that he "had to get locksmith several times to clear locks of cardboard and lucifer match wood shoved into them by 'some evil disposed persons'….so pennies get jammed…".[26]

MARYGATE 30

MARYGATE FROM SCOTS GATE

MARYGATE FROM SCOTS GATE

Scots Gate (earlier names included Scotch Gate, St Mary Gate, New Gate), a Grade I listed building, was formed when the Elizabethan fortifications were constructed between 1577 and 1580, but Marygate (High Street) and what is now Castlegate are much older - the *True Description* map of about 1580 shows these streets built up all the way to the Mary Gate in the Edwardian walls near the castle. In fact, Scots Gate was called the 'New Gate' in 1596-97: "The New Gate. The iron gate here, 'going out of the high towne' to the Mary Gate, needs planking, which with workmanship, will cost by estimation £3 6s 8d".[11] The Gate was widened in 1815 and again in 1858.

Until the A1 bypass of Berwick was opened on 4 November 1983, all the Great North Road traffic passed through this gate. When the lorries were diverted to the new bypass, the first line of the *Berwick Advertiser* report was: "Peace, perfect peace came to the centre of Berwick…"![70]

Marygate (High Street) currently has about 60 listed buildings. Pevsner noted: "[The] Town Hall…it faces up Marygate and here at once the theme is set - a fine town, with closed streets, houses not all of great architectural merit but blending well with each other and the fortifications and the sea. Marygate's unity and compactness have been sadly damaged by the street which cuts into it from the New Bridge, and by the bus station facing it. As nowhere else in the town, the usual rash of cavernous twentieth century shopfronts has spoilt the scene". [40] Pevsner may have been heartened if he had visited later and found that the bus station was no more and that three buildings, sympathetic to the Georgian surrounds, had been built in the resulting space.

Writing about 200 years earlier, in his *History of Berwick-upon-Tweed*, Fuller wrote: "….The principal street….and one through which there is constantly a very considerable thorough-fare, is shameful cramped at the bottom, by the town-hall being injudiciously placed in the middle of it and, near to the other end of the same street, a similar obstruction is occasioned by the building called the Main Guard". [45] Shortly afterwards the Main Guard was relocated adjacent to the Quay Walls (see Section 12).

Looking from above Scots Gate towards Marygate, the first building on the left, the north-east, side is No 124, 'The Elizabethan Town House', built in 1899/1900 as the Avenue Temperance Hotel. In the 1901 Census the owner is given as John Elliot and his wife Mary and two daughters; John's occupation is 'Temperance Hotel Keeper' (and tobacconist!). Their guests at the time came from Batley, Pembroke, Wickham Market in Suffolk, and three from Scotland. By 1911 John

THE ELIZABETHAN TOWN HOUSE, MARYGATE, FROM SCOTS GATE

Elliot was still there, but his wife had died; shortly afterwards the premises was up for sale or let, as the "present tenant, who has established a fine family and commercial connection, is now retiring owing to personal considerations". [71] The building is now a guest house. On the ground floor facing the main street is the Lime Shoe Company, at the side of which is the entrance to Sidey Court.

Nos 122-114 (down to the corner of Walkergate) form a block of early nineteenth century buildings, with later shop fronts. The red, pantiled roofs and tall brick chimney stacks are noticeable, and some shops retain their small 12-paned windows. The block has an endearing wonkiness about it where it has settled over the years. The shops in order are: No 122 Playtime, a toy shop; No 120 Gemini Jewellers; No 118 Taffy's Time Machine for clocks and watches; and Nos 116-114 W. R. Skelly & Son, butchers. This business was 250 years old in 2010; in 1806 Messrs Skelly lived in Backway (modern day Ravensdowne) and had a stall in the Shambles (in Church Street, adjacent to the Town Hall).

Just around the corner in Walkergate, there is a former Baptist Chapel built in 1810 with tall round-headed Georgian windows with fine Gothic tracery; it is now H. B. Longbone's carpet and curtain shop, established in 1946.

On the right, the south-west, side of Marygate, on the corner with Golden Square, Nos 101-109 are listed, eighteenth century, with crow-stepped gables facing Golden Square and incorporating at No 103 Pandora Leaf, jewellers; with same number Glendale Paints; and at 109 the Graduate Beauty Salon. No 113 is nineteenth century, housing the opticians Specsavers; and at No 115 the *Brewers Arms*, early twentieth century - it is shown as licensed in January 1904 and owned/leased by Renton & Co;[71] it has a later Art Deco funnel-shaped glazed front.

Next to the *Brewer's Arms* is Ladbrokes, probably nineteenth century, then the Iceland supermarket at Nos 119-125, occupied for many years by the department store Paxton & Purves, which dated back to 1802, and was incorporated as a limited company in 1908. Mr John Paxton, who founded the firm, had a shop - Linen and Woolen Draper - in the High Street in 1806. By 1894 the store was located at No 125 High Street, and by 1935 at Nos 121-125. The company changed its name to P & P Realisations Ltd in March 1985 when it was purchased by Wilson Distributors (Scotland) Ltd, and was finally dissolved in October 1986. Wilson Distributors (Scotland) Ltd was dissolved itself in 2010.[29]

Under Nos 119-125 there was an archaeological dig before development in 2005-2007, which uncovered a pit, posthole and gully all of medieval date, the pit containing burnt cereal grains, a midden layer with pottery dated fourteenth and fifteenth centuries, and various masonry of medieval date.[3]

The Angels Gift Shop occupies No 127 in a plain nineteenth century building with some rustication lower down. Nos 129-131 are a pair of probably nineteenth century buildings, with Trade Nation games at No 129 and the Fantoosh tea boutique and gifts at No 131.

The present Town Hall replaced an earlier Town House; before that, around 1580, there was what looks like a market cross on the site. The Town Hall is a Grade 1 listed building: "Designed by S & J Worrall, but signed above main entrance by Joseph Dodds, Architect. Front completed in 1754, extended to rear in 1761. Top floor - town gaol."[40] 'The west end has an impressive giant Tuscan portico up a high flight of steps (4 columns), and frieze stating that the building was finished in 1754, restored 1857-8. Entrance doorway under the portico is inscribed 'Joseph Dods. archt.' Surmounted by belfry 150 feet high, similar to Gibbs' St Martin in the Fields. East end facing Church Street/Hide Hill corner has round arches on Tuscan columns, open and with paved butter market underneath on ground floor. The South facade has 4 open arches and 10 arches now closed and occupied by shops. 1st floor contains good Georgian assembly room, with Venetian windows. Top floor has barred windows and housed the town gaol".[36,38]

CASTLEGATE 31

CASTLEGATE FROM SCOTS GATE

CASTLEGATE

Castlegate has about 18 listed buildings. What was left of the medieval church of St Mary was removed when the ramparts were built; Scott wrote that the "Church of St Mary's....placed almost on the site of the present walls on the east side of the street at the present Scotchgate" [51]. The spire is visible of a new St Mary's Church built on Castlegate in 1857-8, the foundation stone being laid on 20 October 1857 and the church consecrated the following year. The church closed in 1989 and the congregation joined that of Holy Trinity; around 1994 the building was converted into residential accommodation.

Looking at the left-hand side of Castlegate, close by Meg's Mount is the Fountain built to commemorate Queen Victoria's Diamond Jubilee in 1897. Beyond the Fountain, Nos 1-23 are all listed as they form a group; they were built between 1837 and 1852 or later, so very late Georgian or early Victorian. No 19, the *Red Lion Public House* was called *The Anglers Cottage Public House* in 1852.

On the right-hand side of Castlegate, beyond B&M, is a worn doorway with inscription including 'renovated 1909'; this is listed as Conduit Head, relating to the 'reservoir' that existed here (in 1852 it was shown as a 'covered reservoir'). The remains of a churchyard were found at its building, most likely connected to the medieval church of St Mary.[51]

A B&M store was opened in 2015, when the previous occupant, a Co-op supermarket, closed its doors. The building, described by Pevsner as 'visually inappropriate but doubtless useful', is on the site of a former chapel, opened in December 1849 as an Independent Church, but taken over by the Baptists from Walkergate Lane in 1858; the chapel was demolished around 1980.

When the Elizabethan fortifications were built, all the buildings close to the new walls in Castlegate were demolished, presumably as a security risk, including the remains of the medieval St Mary's Church. There was still a considerable gap between the Scots Gate and buildings in Castlegate two hundred years later on Armstrong's map of 1769, and it wasn't until after 1837 that buildings appeared on the west side of Castlegate between Meg's Mount and Tweed Street. A map of 1725 shows the area covered currently by B&M and adjoining land stretching along the car park as "Ground belonging to the King whereon stood Houses that were blown up in the late Rebellion 1715", ensuring that the Jacobites wouldn't get too close to the defences. The inhabitants who had lost their houses weren't happy, understandably, and Captain Thomas Phillips, soon to be the engineer in charge of building the barracks, was requested by the Board of Ordnance to list the number and value of houses on Crown land that had been destroyed. The owners themselves valued the land at £815 10s; compensation of £815 seems to have been paid by 1720.

A cattle market was opened on Saturday 23 October 1886 below the walls in what is now the car park; the cattle market had previously been located further up Castlegate since 1848. The new cattle market had 28 pens, accommodating over one thousand cattle. The market continued here until about 1960 when the area became the car park which we see today.

GREENSIDE AVENUE | 32

Greenside Avenue, somtimes called Greenside Place, begins at the side of The Elizabethan Town House on Marygate (See Section 30), built partly on what was a stonemason's yard in the mid-nineteenth century. Next to it are Nos 1-4 St Andrews Place, a modern residential development on the site of St Andrew's Church of Scotland; 1-2 Greenside Avenue are the oldest houses on the Avenue, being early nineteenth century Georgian; beyond them, Nos 3-4 are early twentieth century, built and occupied by October 1908.

> "Joseph Weatherston, was responsible for establishing Greenside Avenue as a new street."

Joseph Weatherston, who lived in the Avenue and in his time was Mayor and Alderman, was responsible for establishing Greenside Avenue as a new street, as well as for building the Avenue Temperance Hotel (now The Elizabethan Town House), the front of which bears his initials - "18 JW 99".

The Trustees of the Scottish Church in Hide Hill resolved in early 1896 to build a new church in Greenside Avenue, at a cost of about £2000, employing a local architect William Gray; there is a drawing of the proposed church in the *Edinburgh Evening News* of Friday 27 March 1896. (71) Building had begun by May that year and St Andrew's Church of Scotland opened in 1897; it was cleared for housing after the church was vacated in 1987 on union with the church in Wallace Green.

GREENSIDE AVENUE FROM ABOVE SCOTS GATE

INFIRMARY, AND VIOLET TERRACE 33

VIOLET TERRACE

BERWICK INFIRMARY

From around 1870 there was discussion about building a new Dispensary and Infirmary to replace the Dispensary at 18 Quay Walls. Tenders were put out in August 1872 and work had started on the building by the end of that year. The Infirmary was completed in 1874. Over the years much has been added to the original building, 'Pastscape' includes a detailed history of the building.[39]

Plans were unveiled in July 2016 to completely rebuild the Infirmary on the same site, but not retaining the original facade including the central bell tower. The building is not listed, but for nearly 150 years has been part of Berwick's skyline, identity and health provision so hopefully the planners will see fit to include at least the facade of the original building in their plans.

Violet Terrace was built 1898-1899, with a total of 12 homes. Previously a Ropery and 'Rope Walk' existed in the ditch between the walls and Well Close/Low Greens area.

On the grassed area in front of the Infirmary is a memorial to Dr Philip Whiteside Maclagan (1818-92), who began practising in Berwick in 1853. After his death the Mayor said: "There were few homes in the community not brightened and cheered by the sunshine of his presence, and there was hardly a man or woman in the community whose life had not been influenced for good, and to some extent elevated and purified by personal contact with the good physician".[71]

VIEW TOWARDS BRASS BASTION

Above the roofline to the north can be seen the old Bell Tower, located on the line of the Edwardian walls. The original Bell Tower was on the north east corner of the fortifications where the remains of Lords Mount are seen today. In 1577 it was rebuilt in an octagonal shape, probably on the foundations of another, round, Edwardian tower in its present location.[11, 2] The bell was rung when border raiders or other enemies were sighted.

HATTERS LANE 34

HATTERS LANE, AUGUST 2015

The photographs show Hatters Lane in August 2015 before demolition of the KwikSave supermarket, and in November of that year after demolition, giving a view through to the library at the corner of Walkergate and Chapel Street. By July 2016 the building of offices on the site was in progress and was completed by the end of that year.

> **"No-one seems to have found any hatters in Hatters Lane. The 1828 Directory names five hatters in the town, but none in Hatters Lane."**

The library was built in 1999-2000 and opened on 14 August 2000; it also housed the social services. The building was refurbished in 2016 and reopened Monday 27 June that year; it now includes Berwick Archives (formerly in Wallace Green) and the Tourist Information Centre (formerly in Marygate), along with other services.

No-one seems to have found any hatters in Hatters Lane. The 1828 Directory names five hatters in the town, but none in Hatters Lane. Hatters Lane does not appear on the *True Description* map of around 1580, but it seems to be in existence by 1725.

HATTERS LANE, NOVEMBER 2015

COLLEGE PLACE 35

COLLEGE PLACE 6 & 8

ST ANDREW'S HOUSE, COLLEGE PLACE

COLLEGE PLACE NOS 6 & 8 AND ST ANDREW'S HOUSE

St Andrews House, College Place, was built as an Infants School and has been in existence from at least 1833; in 1849 about 90 children were being educated there. It ceased as a school around the turn of the century; by 1902 it was described as the 'old British Infants School' and was the Headquarters of the Berwick and District Harriers. It was later used as a church hall for St Andrew's Church of Scotland, Greenside Avenue. It ceased to be the church hall around 1992 when it was converted into a private residence.

The houses in College Place are mainly nineteenth century, stone facades with slate roofs, with No 4 being listed in 2010. Nos 3 and 4 are double-fronted, No 4 having a decorated fanlight in a plain door case. Between Nos 6 & 8 and set back from the building line behind a preserved wall there was previously a Primitive Methodist Chapel and schoolroom, with No 8 College Place being the Manse - a wooden bust above the entrance is said to be that of Dr Lowe, a Methodist Minister.[39] The Chapel seems to have been in existence from about 1829; the first marriage to take place in the chapel after it was licensed (9 July 1855) united William Forrest and Christianna Young in September 1855. The Chapel was described as 'disused' in 1921.[19] The site of the chapel is now part of the new office development being constructed on Walkergate.

COLLEGE PLACE

COXON'S LANE 36

COXON'S LANE, REMAINING WALL OF FORMER GOOD TEMPLARS HALL

COXON'S LANE

Coxon's (earlier named Cookson's) Lane is shown on the *True Description* map of about 1580, built up on both sides, so may well have existed in medieval times.

On the left-hand side of the Lane, behind part of a preserved wall and now used as a car park, is the site of the temperance movement's Good Templars Hall, formally opened on 13 December 1874. Funds had been collected from proceeds of bazaars and such, the cost of building being about £1000. The foundation stone was laid in July 1873; the hall held up to 500 people. "It has a fine pedimented three-bay ashlar front with round-headed door and windows in blank arched recesses".[40]

By walking down to the car park it is possible to look back at the old brickwork of the ramparts themselves, with the bricks being Georgian or earlier. The area between the Good Templars Hall and the ramparts was occupied around the 1950s and 1970s by Henry Moat & Son and later Graham Moat Ltd. The houses on the right of Coxon's Lane are twentieth century, apart from Rampart House on the corner by the ramparts. Rampart House was built about 1799, with alterations in the nineteenth and twentieth centuries; it is a Grade II listed building.

COXON'S LANE, PLAQUE

WALLACE GREEN | 37

WALLACE GREEN, EAST SIDE

WALLACE GREEN, WEST SIDE

Today's neat courtyards, gardens and well-kept houses on the west side of Wallace Green belie the fact that in the mid-nineteenth century the area was a warren of courts and alleys and one of the most unhealthy areas in town. In the Rawlinson report into the health of the town in 1850, Wallace Green was described as one of "those places named as seats of epidemic, endemic, and contagious diseases". A sketch of the housing was included (showing the area covered by current numbers 11 to 21), but "any drawing or written description can only convey a weak description of the actual neglect, filth, wretchedness, and misery palpable to sight and smell…".[50]

The recently vacated Northumberland County Council building on the east side of Wallace Green was built originally as a Court House and Prison, and in use by the end of 1849. Built in a 'Domestic Gothic Style', the section fronting onto Wallace Green held the court room, accommodation for the governor, and chapel, while the cells were in the prison wing at the rear - the small, barred, cell windows can still be seen at the rear today. The building was discontinued as a prison from 1 April 1878, when the criminals, just one male and two females on 29 April, were transferred to Newcastle.

> "Wallace Green was described as one of "those places named as seats of epidemic, endemic, and contagious diseases."

Later, on 11 November 1892, the building opened as the headquarters of the Berwick Urban Sanitary Authority. By 1922 it had become the 'Municipal Buildings', and it was only in June 2016 that it closed as local government offices.

The Gothic church on the left was built for the United Presbyterian congregation from Golden Square; the foundation stone was laid on 2 June 1858 and the church open for worship on 19 June 1859. It was named 'St Andrew's' when the congregation from the former St Andrew's Church of Scotland in Greenside Place joined the congregation in 1986/7.

It is thought that before the Elizabethan walls were built a continuous thoroughfare would have run from Church Street, through Wallace Green to Low Greens. There were proposals over a number of years, culminating in a plan and estimate of cost in 1878, to drive a road through the Ramparts to join up with Low Greens once again, mainly it seems for the benefit of people going to church, but this clearly did not materialise.[7,71]

Part of a building immediately adjacent to the ramparts housed the Berwick Archives until 2015; the corner of the former two cottages seems to be included in an illustration of Holy Trinity Church in Fuller's *History of Berwick-upon-Tweed* of 1799.[45] In 2015 Berwick Archives was moved into temporary accommodation in the Berwick Workspace (behind Marygate and Walkergate), and in July 2016 moved to its new home in the library building in Walkergate. The building in Wallace Green, along with the modern block of offices adjacent - McDonald House - , is now occupied by Northumberland County Council and the Northumbria Healthcare NHS Foundation Trust.

On the west side of the street, Numbers 1-9 form a group, the only listed buildings on this side of Wallace Green; some of the buildings have eighteenth century parts, but are mainly of nineteenth century date. No 1 is in two sections: the rear, with its English bond brickwork, being probably late eighteenth century; and the front early to mid-nineteenth century. No 3 has 16-pane sash windows, pantiled roof and brick chimneys; it was a former restaurant, now residential accommodation. Nos 5, 7 & 9 share a single simple facade, with plain oblong fanlights; part of this building was *The Masons' Arms* in 1852.

No 11 was built after 1873 as an addition to the hall at the rear - the Wallace Green Mission Hall, which was opened in December 1873. It was recently used as council committee rooms, and is now the Wallace Green Hall guest house. The style of the facade is quite different from the surrounding buildings. No 13 seems always to have had a narrow frontage, with an access passage to the rear; Nos 15 & 17 share a modern facade. Nos 19 and 21, more substantial houses, have slate roofs, brick chimneys and are probably early nineteenth century.

38 LOOKING BACK ALONG THE WALLS, AND THE CHURCHYARD

LOOKING BACK TOWARDS CUMBERLAND BASTION AND HOSPITAL

On the far right, with the pantiled roof and white rendering, can be seen No 89 Low Greens, in former times the Fishers Arms, a nineteenth century public house dating from at least 1841; it was originally two houses but was rebuilt in its present form about the end of the nineteenth century. It continued as a public house until at least July 1954, and is now a private residence.

39 FROM BRASS BASTION

HAVEN BERWICK HOLIDAY PARK AND MAGDALENE FIELDS GOLF CLUB

At the very top north west corner of the golf course on Northumberland Avenue, and just outside the line of the medieval walls, was situated the medieval hospital of St Mary Magdalen; Magdalen (Maudlin) Fields takes its name from the hospital. The hospital, for the poor, was founded around the end of the thirteenth century and continued until at least midway through the fifteenth century. Some coffin lids and other fragments have been found in the area, but the exact location of the hospital is unknown. Until at least 1938 the site was included on Ordnance Survey maps.

The Magdalene Fields Golf Club course was opened as a nine hole course around May 1903, but previously in October 1889 a golf club had been formed in Berwick but it was decided to play at Goswick; the club there was originally called the Berwick-upon-Tweed Golfing Club, but later, and to this day, was called the Berwick-upon-Tweed (Goswick) Golf Club. A nine-hole course was opened in Goswick in April 1890 and extended to 18-holes in 1894.[59]

GOLF COURSE, CLUB HOUSE AND OCEAN BEYOND

From the outset the Magdalene Fields Golf Club welcomed both male and female members; there were a couple of early attempts to form an 18-hole course but it was finally extended to 18 holes in 1973 when it wrapped itself around the caravan park. There were problems with the site - it wasn't until 1967 that grazing cattle were at last removed; until then the greens were surrounded by barbed wire and the cattle were not averse to eating golf balls: "one member saw two new balls, which had cost him 5/- each, eaten up by cattle before he had even completed the first hole!". Fog and the haar are other recurring problems, but in 1999 one Willie Thompson managed a hole-in-one in thick fog![58]

From later nineteenth century into the twentieth an isolation hospital, the Port Hospital, (later the Infectious Diseases Hospital) existed in the ditch between the modern Lord's Mount housing development and the remains of the Edwardian walls. The stanks (ditch) to the south has been used as a football pitch for over a hundred years.

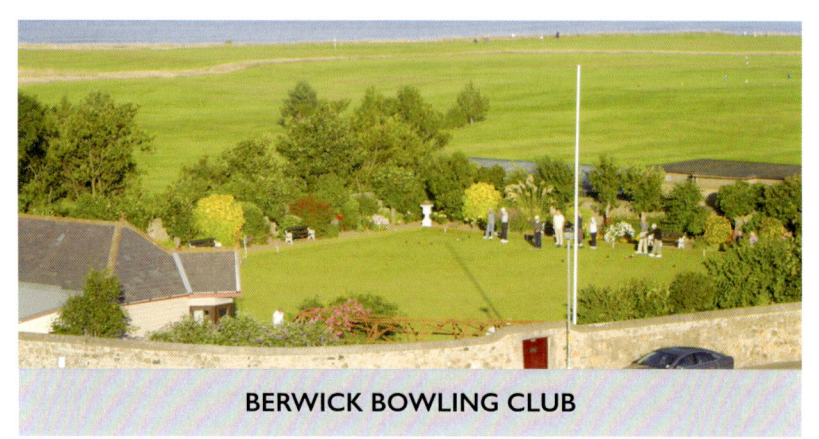

BERWICK BOWLING CLUB

Bowling in the evening sunlight! The Berwick-upon-Tweed Bowling Club dates back to at least 1870. In 1894 the club was looking for a new site for a green (at that time the green was on Ravensdowne) and agreed to acquire three quarters of an acre on Pier Field from the Duke of Northumberland at a rent of £8 per annum; the estimated cost of laying the green was £600. The new green was opened in the following year, with the Club reconstituted as the Berwick Bowling Club; it is shown on 1897 Ordnance Survey map in its present location, complete with trees surrounding the site.

VIEW TOWARDS WINDMILL BASTION

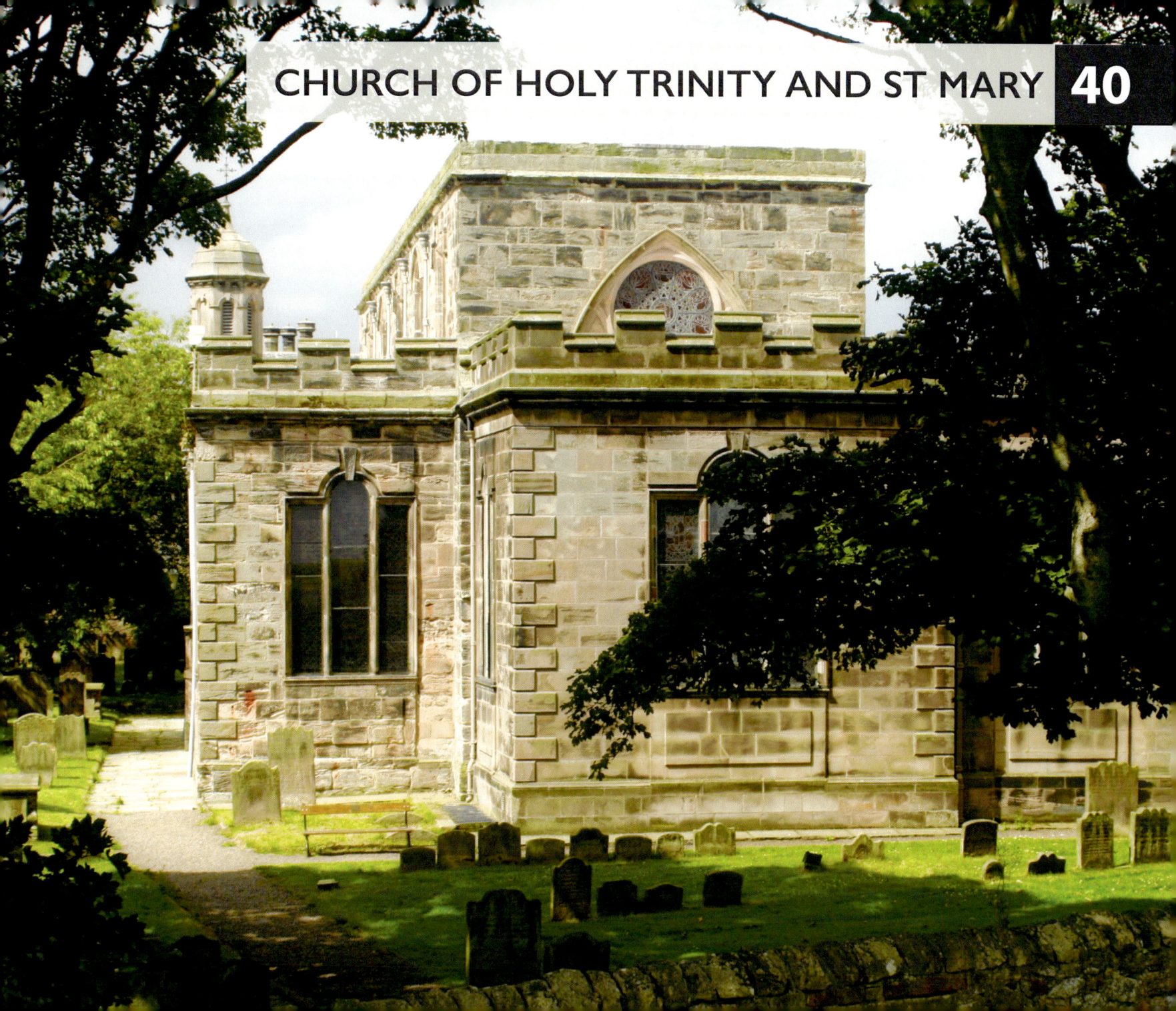

CHURCH OF HOLY TRINITY AND ST MARY 40

PARISH CHURCH OF HOLY TRINITY & ST MARY

The parish church of Holy Trinity, "a building of quite exceptional architectural interest",[40] was built between 1650 and 1652, during the Cromwellian Commonwealth. It replaced a medieval church of the same name founded in the twelfth century, which it is believed was situated to the south of the present church. The *'True Description…'* plan of about 1580 shows a narrow, aisleless church with probably slate roof, very close to the site of the present church; it shows a large cross at the east end, but no tower or spire.[60] In June 1584 the Mayor of Berwick petitioned Queen Elizabeth thus: "That it might please her Majestie to grant some money to the building of a new church in Berwick, the old being very small and in utter ruin ready to fall, not able to hold the sixth part of the inhabitants, so that in tyme of Godes devine service, the greater sorte of people do bestowe themselves in alehowses and other places—and when they are taken and presented, they altogether excuse themselves for lacke of roome in the churche".[11] When the stone bridge was built in the time of James I, the money given was for a bridge and a church, but by the time the bridge was finished and paid for there was only £39 18s 6d left for a church, hardly enough for a wayside cross!

Money was raised eventually and, mainly at the instigation of the Governor George Fenwick, building began around 1650, the builder being a master-mason, John Young from Blackfriars in London. Stone, wood and lead from the castle was used to build the church, among other structures. The church opened for worship in 1652 and it was consecrated in 1662. The building was in a plain, Puritan, style: there was "no altar, steeple, chancel, stained glass, bells, font or organ".[73] A font was installed in 1662, and an organ in 1772/1773; in the days before electricity, on 15 November 1805 William Thomas was chosen as 'Bellows-Blower to the Organ' for the parish Church (after death of his predecessor William Ord).[71] The chancel was added in 1855, one of several changes to the original building in that year. At different times there were galleries on each side of the church but only that on the west side remains today. The windows are three-light of the 'Venetian' style; there was earlier a Gothic window at the west end which was replaced by the present 'Venetian' window in keeping with the other windows. The gate posts leading from the Parade, which are listed in their own right, date from 1750.[40,73]

When St Mary's Parish Church in Castlegate closed in 1989, the congregation joined with Holy Trinity, which was then renamed Holy Trinity and St Mary.

COWPORT 41

COWPORT

THE PARADE

A 'Cowgate Tower' existed in the old Edwardian walls, thought to be named thus as a way to lead cattle out of town to pasture beyond the walls. Cowport (earlier Cow Port, Cow Port Gate….) was one of the original Elizabethan gates into the town; on the *True Description* map of about 1580 it seems to be shown as a gap in the walls as though incomplete, but the map does show the Edwardian Cowgate Tower as still standing and in use; the Elizabethan Cowgate was completed by 1596.[60] In a letter of that year from Sir Robert Carey to Lord Burghley: "The new Cow gate called "Carey porte," and bridge over the "stanck" there, 498l. 4s. 9d".[11]

The gate had a portcullis, and the present wooden doors date from mid-eighteenth century, according to Pevsner.[40] Beside the gate is a Gatekeepers Lodge (called a guardhouse by Pevsner), dated above the doorway as 1755.

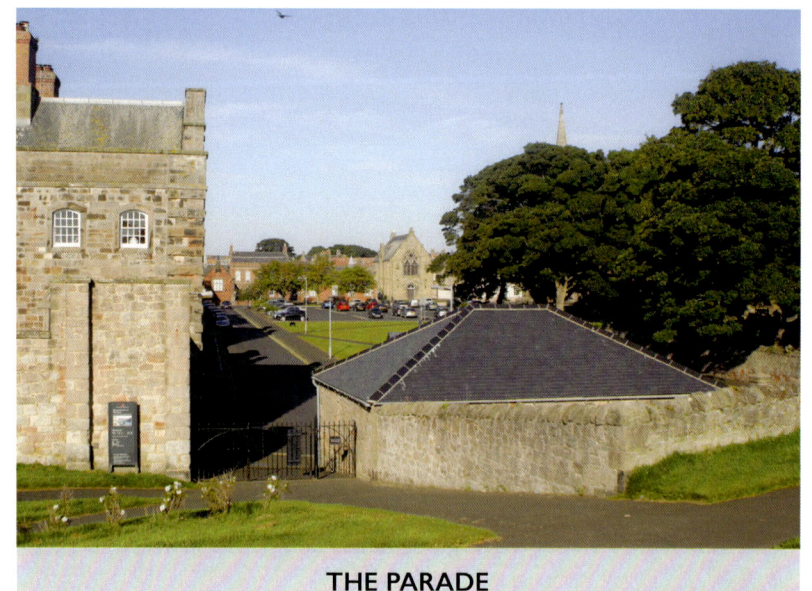

THE PARADE

BARRACKS 42

BARRACKS GATEHOUSE

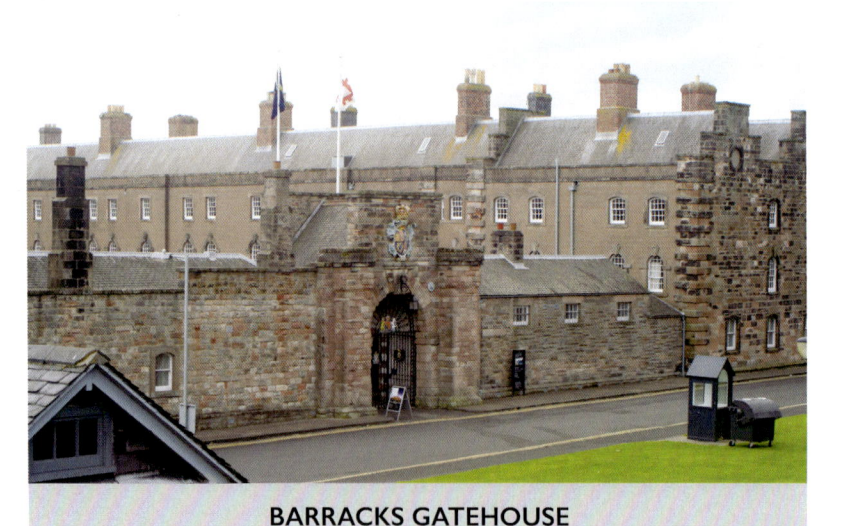

In the 'Earl of Pembroke Collection' in the Wiltshire Record Office there is a sketch dated 1717 of the proposed Ravensdowne Barracks; the drawing is attributed to Nicholas Hawksmoor, who had some influence on the buildings of the Board of Ordnance between 1715 and 1724, including the Barracks we see today.[34] The Barracks were begun in 1717, shortly after the Jacobite rebellion of 1715, and were first occupied in 1721. The local inhabitants no doubt breathed a sigh of relief as before this the soldiers were billeted in local inns and houses!

On 9th March 1717 "draughts and estimates of the Barracks ordered by his Majesty to be built at Berwick for the reception of 36 officers and 600 men, amounting to upwards of £4900" was noted in the Board of Ordnance minutes, with the intention of beginning the work that summer.[9] The foundations were begun in July; as to materials, the bricks were obtained locally but the timber was imported from Norway. The two main accommodation blocks were virtually complete by 22nd March 1720: "…the 2 piles of Barracks at Berwick are finished and furnished with Beddsteads, Formes, Tables etc and that Bedding is contracted for, and that tonges, fire shovells etc will be sent from hence, and the Undertakers for performing the outward works of the said Barracks are to proceed in compleating the same according to the last year's estimate".[9]

The resulting building was not exactly to Hawksmoor's drawing; his designs were later amended and simplified by the military engineer in charge of building, Captain Thomas Phillips, but the building substantially follows Hawksmoor's ideas with its general layout of storeys and windows, its elongated quoins and crow-stepped gables.[34] The windows vary in design, some are rounded with emphasised key-stones, some flattened and others flat.

The main entrance and the east and west blocks were built in the first phase from 1717; the south block, called the 'Clock Block' for obvious reasons, was built much later, between 1739 to 1741 (the east end of the Clock Block has a striking central round-arched doorway with very large fanlight with side windows). The exterior walls of the buildings are stone, but for the interior skin and chimney stacks, bricks are employed. On 18 October 1717 it was "Proposed that John Tully upon his petition has the liberty to break as much ground in the common moors of Tweedmouth on the east side of Eytill [Etal] way as will afford sufficient quantity of clay to make 600,000 bricks for the service of the Barracks and that upon Mr Mayor's motion the other workmen employed by Capt Philips for making bricks for the same purposed have like liberty for a like quantity of ground in a convenient part of the said moor filling up the ground they dig so as to prevent any danger that may happen by the grounds being open".[8]

The barracks were closed for accommodating soldiers at the end of January 1964. Currently the east block houses two museums: the Regimental Museum of the King's Own Scottish Borderers; and the 'By Beat of Drum' museum - opened in May 1985 by the Duchess of Gloucester - telling the story of the infantryman of the British Army

106

BARRACKS FROM SOUTH EAST

from 1660 to 1900. The west block is unused; and the south block, the Clock Block, houses the Berwick-upon-Tweed Museum and Art Gallery. The former gymnasium, built in 1901, between the east block and the ramparts, is the Gymnasium Gallery, exhibiting contemporary art. The former guardhouse, complete with barred windows (on the right of the main entrance looking from outside) is the entrance to the complex and is also the English Heritage shop.

43 VIEWS, AND WINDMILL BASTION

LOOKING BACK TOWARDS BRASS BASTION

LOOKING BACK TOWARDS BRASS BASTION

There was a Windmill Tower on the old Edwardian walls near the present Windmill Bastion, so the latter was probably named after it; there is a depiction of a windmill on John Speed's map of late sixteenth or early seventeenth century, but none since. It would have been an excellent spot for a windmill with the almost constant supply of wind from the river and the sea!

VIEW FROM WINDMILL BASTION, INCLUDING COASTGUARD TOWER

BEACON ON WINDMILL BASTION, WITH INSET ON QUEEN'S 90TH BIRTHDAY 21 APRIL 2016

The Coastguard Watch Tower was built in 1964, about the time the Coastguard Station on the hill behind Pier Road closed (See Section 46). When the Coastguard was withdrawn the tower was initially unused, but it was reopened in November 2003 by volunteers who scan the seas on a part-time basis.

44 MAGAZINE

The Magazine was built 1749-1750 to store gunpowder barrels. If there was an accident the massive buttresses were designed to force any explosion upwards. Thankfully, it was never tested; the inhabitants of the nearby Lions House were surely grateful for that! Even on such a utilitarian building an attempt was made for some style, with the pediments on the outer wall and over the doorway of the Magazine itself.

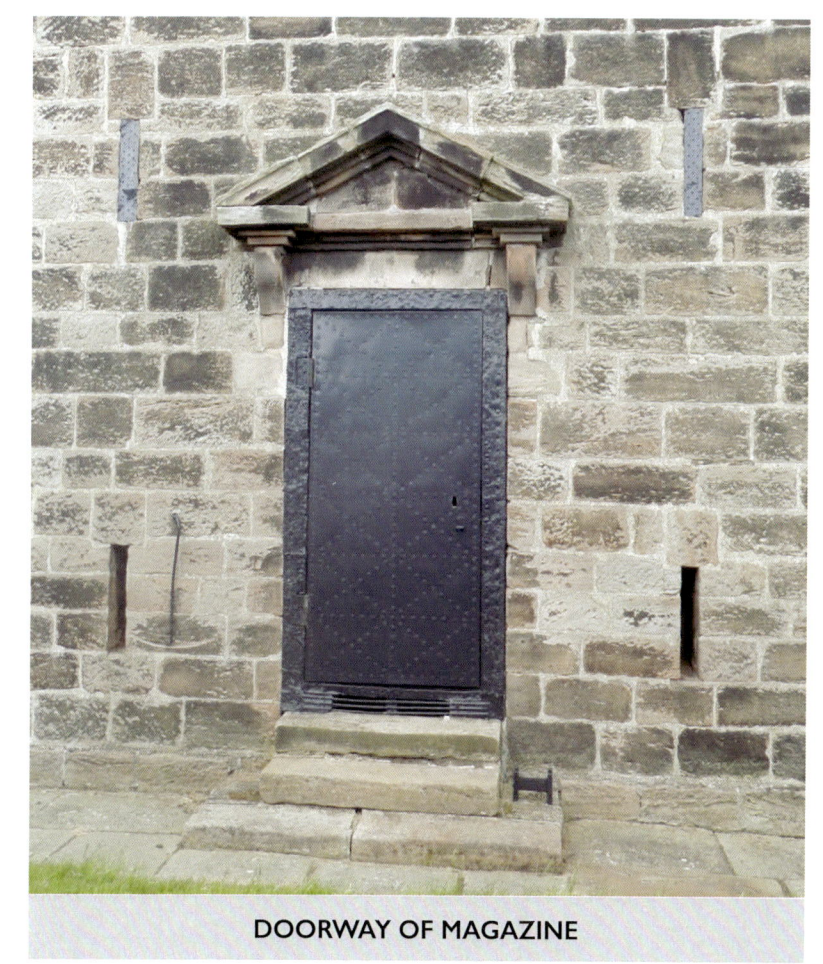

MAGAZINE INTERIOR (REPRODUCED WITH PERMISSION)

DOORWAY OF MAGAZINE

45 LIONS HOUSE AND ALLOTMENTS

ALLOTMENTS AND ICE HOUSE

Close to the Magazine is the impressive Lions House, with its symmetrical classical proportions and its 'rising sun' fanlight design; and, of course, its two seated lions on the gateposts guarding the house, described by Pevsner as "endearingly ill-carved" and that "leer cheekily".[40] The house, early nineteenth century, appears on Wood's map of 1822, owned by the 'late T.F. Curry'. The house was presented to the Berwick Preservation Trust in 1972 for restoration; the work was carried out "through the generosity of three local businessmen – Tom and Robert Gladstone and Jim Mulhern".[31] The house formed the subject of one of Lowry's paintings. It is thought that at one time he considered purchasing the property.

Although the plot of land that the allotments now cover has been under cultivation since at least the eighteenth century, the allotments themselves date from before February 1921 when "Allotment Gardens, Rope Walk, Ice Houses and three Dwelling Houses [and] nearly two and a half acres" were put up for sale, the allotment tenancies being on three months notice. The advertisement, in the *Berwickshire News and General Advertiser*, suggested that the site was "ripe for de-

ALLOTMENTS, WITH TWEEDMOUTH AND SPITTAL ON HORIZON

velopment as Building Site or Market Garden".[71] As the soil is so rich, it is thought that the site was originally one of the town's middens.

In 1822 there was a bowling green on the site, and a rope works on the rise across the ground from the walls to immediately below the ice house, which is also shown on that map. The rope works, or ropery, was still shown on the map of 1922, on the line of the Cat Well Wall, from King's Mount to Meg's Mount, that was part of the fortifications from the 1570s, abandoned before completion.

46 KING'S MOUNT, AND BACK TO NESS GATE

COASTGUARD STATION COTTAGES AND COASTLINE

VIEW TOWARDS TWEEDMOUTH, INCLUDING THE LIFEBOAT STATION

The Coastguard Station Cottages was the town's Coastguard Station, replacing an early one on King's Mount. It was in course of construction in May 1878, when the masons went on strike for more wages and shorter hours. When completed it was staffed by a chief officer and six men - in 1881, at No 1 with the lookout window, lived the Chief Officer, HM Coastguard, Hugh McLoughlin; it was in use as a Coastguard Station until around 1964.[71]

The cricket ground behind Devon Terrace and Coastguard Station Cottages pre-dates 1849, so there has been the sound of leather on willow for over 160 years, and long may it continue!

On the south side of the river, seen between the chimneys of Long-

VIEW TOWARDS NESS GATE AND FISHER'S FORT

stone View, is the present Lifeboat Station, opened on Carr Rock in April 1941, but in danger of being closed as an economy measure in 2016.

Which brings us back to Ness Gate……….

SOURCES

Archaeology

1. Archaeologia Aeliana [Society of Antiquaries of Newcastle upon Tyne]. 5th Series, Vol XXVII, 1999. "Excavations at the New Quay, Berwick-upon-TWeed, 1996". By W.B. Griffiths, pp 75-108. Includes Bibliography pp 106-108.

2. Archaeologia Aeliana : or miscellaneous tracts relating to antiquity. 5th Series, Vol 28/2000, 163. Paterson, Caroline: The Bell Tower at Berwick-upon-Tweed. 163-75

2a. Archaeological Data Service; an integrated online catalogue indexing over 1.3 million records. http://archaeologydataservice.ac.uk/archsearch/

3. Berwick-upon-Tweed: Northumberland Extensive Urban Survey. Northumberland County Council and English Heritage, 2009. http://www.northumberland.gov.uk/WAMDocuments/0CC30F22-6C33-4AAF-A6BB-BC75AB2453F1_1_0.pdf?nccredirect=1. From archaeological angle.

4. Derham, K. Distribution and significance of urban waterlogged deposits in Berwick-upon-Tweed. Northumberland County Council and English Heritage, Nov 2013. Project 3A5.201). https://content.historicengland.org.uk/images-books/publications/berwick-upon-tweed-distribution-significance-urban-waterlogged-deposits/6509_Berwick_UDM_report.pdf/

5. John Dewar's Granary, Dewar's Lane, Berwick-upon-Tweed, Headland Archaeology, 2004. [Event 13306]

6. National Monuments Record Excavation Index. See http://www.heritage-gateway.org.uk/Gateway/

Archives & Libraries

7. Berwick Archives - http://www.experiencewoodhorn.com/berwick-record/ Includes full range of archival sources for the area, including borough, business, court, estate and church records, maps, planning applications, directories, electoral registers, newspapers etc. The online catalogue includes only some records; speak with the archivist and consult the printed Handlist.

8. Berwick-upon-Tweed Guild Minutes and other minutes. (Berwick Archives)

9. Board of Ordnance Minutes, National archives, Ref WO 47.

10. British Library group of online catalogues, including 'Explore' the main British Library Catalogue (http://explore.bl.uk/primo_library/libweb/action/search.do?dscnt=1&dstmp=1443853625111&vid=BLVU1&fromLogin=true)

11. Calendar of Border Papers. http://www.british-history.ac.uk/search?query=&title=Calendar+of+Border+Papers+ (and Berwick Library and Berwick Archives)

12. Census Returns (Berwick Archives & Berwick Library)

13. Defoe, Daniel. A tour through England and Wales, Vols 1 & 2. J. M. Dent, 1928.

14. Directories (Berwick Archives & Berwick Library) - various dates

15. Electoral Registers (Berwick Archives and Berwick Library) - various dates

16. English Heritage group of online databases on historic buildings and sites: National Monuments Record (NMR) (http://pastscape.english-heritage.org.uk/). Gives descriptions and history of sites and buildings, lists any excavations or surveys that have taken place, and gives links to maps and other websites.

Images of England (http://www.imagesofengland.org.uk/) Gives images and text for most of the listed buildings in England; the text is mainly architectural information about the buildings. N.B. The database shows buildings and information up to 2001 only. For details of buildings listed since then see English Heritage's National Heritage List (http://historicengland.org.uk/listing/the-list/)

English Heritage Archives (http://www.englishheritagearchives.org.uk/). Photographs and documents on England's historic buildings and archaeological sites.

Heritage Gateway (http://www.heritagegateway.org.uk/gateway/) Searches across national and local records of England's historic sites and buildings. e.g. leads to National Heritage List; to NMR's Pastscape, and to NMR Excavation Index.

Viewfinder (http://viewfinder.english-heritage.org.uk/) Photographs from 1850s held on the NMR.

17. The First(-Twentieth) Volume of the Wren Society 1924(-1943). [Edited by Arthur T. Bolton and H. D. Hendry. With portraits.]. vol. 18. The Wren MS. 'Court Orders.' With a supplement of official papers from the Public Record Office, Welbeck Abbey, etc. pp. 204. pl. XXV. 1941. Wren Society (LONDON) 1924.
18. Friends of Berwick and District Museum and Archives. http://www.berwickfriends.org.uk
19. London Gazette. https://www.thegazette.co.uk. Last 350 years searchable.
20. National Archives. (http://www.nationalarchives.gov.uk/default.htm). 'Discovery' database holds more than 32 million descriptions of records held by The National Archives and more than 2,500 archives across the country.
21. National Library of Scotland catalogues. http://www.nls.uk.
22. Northumberland County Archives: http://www.experiencewoodhorn.com/collections/
23. Northumberland County Library catalogue and digital resources: http://mylibrary.co.uk
24. Online Directories (http://specialcollections.le.ac.uk/cdm/landingpage/
25. Queen Victoria's Journals. http://www.queenvictoriasjournals.org
26. Sanitary Authority Minutes, No IX, Sept 1897-July 1990. Berwick Archives Ref E1/9.

Art

27. Bowes, Edwin. Artists in Berwick: inspiration and celebration. Berwick upon Tweed: Berwick upon Tweed Preservation Trust, 2009. ISBN 978-0-9552109-7-6.

Biography

28. Dictionary of National Biography. http://www.oxforddnb.com/public/index.html. Also a copy in the Berwick Library Reserve Collection.

Buildings, architecture

29. A descriptive account of Berwick-upon-Tweed. Illustrated. Berwick-upon-Tweed Borough Council, 1995. ISBN 0952673800. Berwick in 1894 & 1994.
30. Berwick-upon-Tweed Conservation Area. Berwick-upon-Tweed Borough Council, March 2008. http://www.northumberland.gov.uk/WAMDocuments/13E8CC20-1692-4697-B510-3F6F579924CF_1_0.pdf?nccredirect=1
31. Berwick Preservation Trust. http://www.berwick-pt.co.uk/Initial/Opening_fs.htm
32. Buildings Study Group of Berwick Civic Society. Made particular study of the buildings in Bridge Street. http://berwickcivicsociety.org.uk/building-study/
33. Heritage Gateway (http://www.heritagegateway.org.uk/gateway/). Searches across national and local records of England's historic sites and buildings. e.g. leads to listed buildings (information similar to 'Images of

England' data, to National Monuments Record (NMR) Pastscape, and to NMR Excavation Index.

34. Hewlings, Richard: Hawksmoor's 'Brave Designs for the Police'. IN: English architecture public and private: essays for Kerry Downes / edited by John Bold and Edward Chaney. London : Hambledon, 1993., pp 215-229. ISBN 1852850957.

35. Historic Buildings of Berwick. A Berwick Civic Society Heritage Leaflet. www.berwickcivicsociety.org.uk

36. Images of England website: http://www.imagesofengland.org.uk. Gives images and text for most of the listed buildings in England; the text is mainly architectural information about the buildings. N.B. The database shows buildings and information up to 2001 only. For details of buildings listed since then see English Heritage's National Heritage List (http://historicengland.org.uk/listing/the-list/)

37. Keys to the Past (Northumberland Historic Environment Record). http://www.keystothepast.info/Pages/Home.aspx

38. National Heritage List (http://historicengland.org.uk/listing/the-list/). Details of current listed buildings, text only; for photographs (to 2001 only) see 'Images of England' http://www.imagesofengland.org.uk

39. Pastscape. https://pastscape.org.uk/default.aspx. Includes details of buildings that have been refused listing, with reasons. Also details of c 152 wrecks off Berwick.

40. Pevsner, N & Richmond, I. Northumberland. [The Buildings of England series]. Newhaven and London: Yale University Press, 2002. ISBN 978 0 300 09638 5

41. Planning Applications. https://publicaccess.northumberland.gov.uk/online-applications//search.do?action=simple. Database covers about 20-30 years. For earlier planning applications, consult Berwick Archives.

42. Strang, C.A. Borders and Berwick: an illustrated architectural guide to the Scottish Borders and Tweed Valley. Rutland Press, 1994. ISBN 1 873190 10 7. pp 5-19.

History, Berwick-upon-Tweed

43. Berwick Time Lines. http://berwicktimelines.tumblr.com

44. Cowe, F. M. Berwick-upon-Tweed: a short historical guide. Berwick: J.D. Cowe, 1998 (revised edition). ISBN 09533130X.

45. Fuller, John. The History of Berwick-upon-Tweed. Third Edition. Newcastle-upon-Tyne: Frank Graham, 1973. SBN 902833081. [First edition 1799].

46. Good, J. A Directory and Concise History of Berwick-upon-Tweed. Berwick-upon-Tweed: W Lockhead, 1806.

47. Johnstone, Thomas. The History of Berwick-upon-Tweed (1817). Facsimile edition published by Berwick History Society, 2004.

48. Lamont-Brown, Raymond. The life and times of Berwick-upon-Tweed. John Donald Publishers, 1988. ISBN 0859762335.

49. Menuge, A. Berwick-upon-Tweed: three places, two nations, one town. Swindon: English Heritage, 2009. ISBN 978 1 84802 029 0.

50. Rawlinson, R. Report to the General Board of Health on a Preliminary Enquiry into the Sewerage, Drainage and Supply of Water, and the Sanitary Condition of the Inhabitants of the Parish of Berwick-upon-Tweed. London: W Clowes & Son, 1850.

51. Scott, J. Berwick-upon-Tweed: the History of the Town and Guild. London: E Stock, 1888.

52. Walker, J. Berwick-upon-Tweed then & now. Stroud: Tempus, 1999. ISBN 0752418521. Illustrated.

53. Walker, J. Berwick-upon-Tweed. (Images of England series). Stroud: Tempus, 1998. ISBN 0752415174. Illustrated.

54. Walker, J. Berwick-upon-Tweed through time. Stroud: Amberley, 2009. ISBN 9781848685604. Illustrated.

55. Walking the Walls: Berwick-upon-Tweed and its fortifications. Berwick-upon-Tweed Civic Society, 2011. 8 page leaflet.

History, General

56. British History Online. http://www.british-history.ac.uk

Leisure

57. Chopwell Woodland Park: http://www.forestry.gov.uk/chopwell
58. Langmack, Tony. Magdalene Fields Golf Club…the first 100 years. Berwick-upon-Tweed: Tony Langmack, 2003.
59. McCreath, Bill. History of the Berwick-upon-Tweed (Goswick) Golf Club, 1889-1989. Berwick-upon-Tweed (Goswick) Golf Club, 1990.

Maps

60. A highly finished coloured plan or bird's eye view of Berwick upon Tweed, entitled, "The True Description of Her Majesties town of Barwick", drawn about 1580. See Cotton Ms. Titus C.XIII, Cotton Ms. Titus F.XIII. Article 36, and Harley Ms. 151.[Held in the British Library].
61. Berwick Pier Railway map, 1824. Available from British Library: http://explore.bl.uk/primo_library/libweb/action/search.do?vid=BLVU1. Map reproduced on page 74 of Menuge (see Source 49 above). British Library, Map 18.c.13 (127-132). http://explore.bl.uk/
62. Ordnance Survey and other maps: Berwick Archives and Berwick Library.
63. Ordnance Survey Large-Scale Town Plan, 1852, and other maps. [http://maps.nls.uk/townplans/berwick.html]. Later Ordnance Survey Maps, various dates.

Maritime

64. Barrow, Tony. The Whaling Trade of North-East England, 1750-1850. University of Sunderland Press, 2001. ISBN 187375783-2.
65. Berwick shipyard. http://www.berwickshipyard.com/ Comprehensive database on the subject.
66. Morris, Jeff. An Illustrated guide to our lifeboat stations. Part 1: Berwick to the Humber…. 1986.

Military

67. History of the King's Works.
   Vol I. The Middle Ages. HMSO, 1963. pp 1-552
   Vol II. The Middle Ages HMSO, 1963. pp 553-1139.
   Vol IV (Part II) 1485-1660. HMSO 1982. ISBN 0116708328.
   [Copies in Berwick Library, etc]
68. Pattison, Paul. Berwick Barracks and fortifications. London: English Heritage, 2011. 9781848020740.

Monuments

69. Public Monuments and Sculpture Association: http://www.pmsa.org.uk/pmsa-database/9816/

Newspapers

70. Berwick Advertiser: http://www.berwick-advertiser.co.uk
71. British Newspaper Archive (http://www.britishnewspaperarchive.co.uk) - includes coverage of Berwick Advertiser and Berwickshire News and General Advertiser
72. Newspapers on microfilm in Berwick Archives and Berwick Library.

Religious Houses, Churches

73. Berwick Parish Church: a Commonwealth Church, 1652-2002. Berwick: Parish Church Trust, 2002.
74. Cowan, I B and Easson, D E, 1976. Medieval Religious Houses in Scotland. 2nd Edition, Longmans, London.
75. Knowles, David. Medieval religious houses, England and Wales, by David Knowles and R. Neville Hadcock. Longman, 1971. 0582112303. Lists individual priories, etc. Groups Orders together.
76. Macewen, Alexander R. Life & Letters of John Cairns. London: Hodder & Stoughton, 1895.

INDEX

Albert, Prince 75
Allotments 113
Angels Gift Shop 80
Anglers Cottage Public House 82
Art galleries 49, 74, 107
Art Studio, Marlin Buildings 27
Audela 39
Avenue, The 15-17
Avenue Temperance Hotel 79, 84

B & M Store 82
Bank Alley 63
Bank Hill (Bankhill) 17, 70-72
Baptist Church 69, 80, 82
Barrels Inn 61
Barracks, The 22, 105-107
Bay Terrace 10-12
Bay View 25
Beacon, Windmill Bastion, 109
Bell Tower (on Edwardian walls) 86
Berwick Amateur Rowing Club 69
Berwick & District Harriers 90
Berwick Archives 88, 95
Berwick Bowling Club 100
Berwick Breweries 22
Berwick Bridge 56-58, 67
Berwick Cycles 47
Berwick Library 88
Berwick Pier Railway 7

Berwick Preservation Trust 44, 49, 51, 53, 69, 76
Berwick Theatre 42
Berwick Tourist Information Centre 88
Berwick-upon-Tweed (Goswick) Golf Club 99-100
Berwick-upon-Tweed Museum & Art Gallery 107
Berwick Urban Sanitary Authority 95
Berwick Whale Fishing Company 31
Berwick Youth Hostels Association 48-49
Billiard Room 25
Bishop of Durham 57-58
Black Watch Tower 5
Board of Ordnance 22, 106
Boathouse 69
Border Breweries Ltd 22
Bower Villa 24
Bowling Club, Berwick-upon-Tweed 100
Bowling Greens 25, 100, 113
Brass Bastion 98-100
Brewers Arms 80
Bridge End 59-61, 63
Bridge Gate 55, 57
Bridge House 60-61
Bridge Street 47, 51, 60
Bridge Terrace 62-64
Bridges 28, 56-58, 60, 65-67, 73-76
Briggate 47, 51, 60
British & Foreign School Society 29
British School, The 29
Building Study Group 47

Bulwark in the Sands 27
Burrell, James, Bridge Master 57-58
By Beat of Drum Museum 106

Cairns, John 31
Call family 17
Cannon, Russian 19
Carmelite Friary 11, 17
Carr & Co 22
Carr Rock 7, 27, 116
Castlegate 78, 81-82
Cat Well Wall 12, 63, 113
Cattle market 82
Chandlery, The 38-39
Chapel of Ravensdale 60-61, 63
Chopwell Forest [& Woodland Park] 57
Church of Holy Trinity & St Mary 31, 82, 101-102
Churches 31, 69, 70-71, 72, 74, 80, 82, 84, 90
Cinema 42
Cleet Court 8-9, 12
Coaches 41-42
Coal seam 67
Coastguard Cottages 20, 114-115
Coastguard Station 20, 109, 114-115
Coastguard Watch Tower 109
College Place 89-90
Collingwood House 53
Conduit Head 82
Congregation of Protestant Dissenters 71

Co-op Supermarket 82
Corn Exchange, The 42
Corporation Academy 69
Court House and Prison 94-95
Cowport 103-104
Coxon's Lane 91-92
Coxon's Tower 26-27
Cricket Ground 115
Custom House 36-37, 44, 55
Customs Watch House 27

Darling, Grace 12
Deer antlers, red 67
Defoe, Daniel 58
Devon Terrace 20, 115
Dewar's Lane Granary 48-49
Dickens, Charles 42
Dispensary 37, 86
Dixon, John 20, 31
Dominican friars 60-61
Domus Dei 55, 61
Domus Pontis 61

East Coast Line 66
Elizabethan Town House 79, 84
Elliot, John 79
English Estates North 39
English Gate 55, 57

Fishers Arms Inn, The 41, 97
Fisher's Fort 18-20,
Flag Lieutenant, The 42
Flagstaff House 17
Flying Scotsman 73, 76

Forfarshire 12
Fountain, Queen Victoria Jubilee 82
Friaries 11, 17, 60-61, 63
Friars of the Sack 60-61
Friary, Carmelite 11, 17

Gaol 74, 94-95
Gemini Jewellers 80
Glendale Paints 80
Golden Square 69, 80
Golden Swan Inn, The 41
Golf Club, The Berwick-upon-Tweed
    (Goswick) 99-100
Golf Club, The Magdalen Fields 99-100
Good, Thomas Sword 35
Good Templars Hall 91-92
Governor's House and Gardens 21-22, 24
Graduate Beauty Salon 80
Graham Moat Ltd 92
Grammar School (Old) 13-14, 69
Granaries 42, 49, 53, 63-64
Granary Gallery 49
Great North Road 79
Greenside Avenue 83-84
Gymnasium Gallery 107

Harbour Commissioners 20
Harriers, Berwick & District 90
Harrison, George 20
Hatters Lane 87-88
Hawkesmoor, Nicholas 22, 106
Hen & Chickens Hotel, The 41
Henry Moat & Son 92
Hide Hill 42

Holloway Bros 67
Holy Island 75-76
Holy Island children 29
Hospitals 14, 60-61, 99, 100

Ice House 37, 68-69, 113
Iceland Supermarket 80
Independent Church 82
Infants School 90
Infirmary 85-86

Jerningham, Lady 71-72
Jerningham, Sir Hubert 71-72
Jimmy Strength 7, 25, 35
Johnson & Darlings Ltd 22, 63

Kemble, Stephen 42
Kingdom Hall 74
King's Arms Hotel, The 41-42
King's Mount 5, 7, 12
Kipper Hill 9
KwikSave Supermarket 88

Ladbrokes 80
Leaping Salmon, The 68-69
Leith, William 20
Leper hospital 14
Library 88
Lifeboat Station 14, 27, 116
Lime Shoes Company 79-80
Limekilns 5
Lindisfarne Ltd 22
Lindisfarne Homes Ltd 22
Lionel & Clarissa 42

Lions House 112-113
London & Berwick Tavern, The 41
Longbone, H.B. 80
Longstone Lighthouse 5
Longstone View 4-5, 115
Loovre, The 74-76
Love Lane 60, 62-64
Lowry, L.S. 49, 61, 113
Lowry's at the Chandlery 39
Lynwood House 17

Maclagan, Dr Philip Whiteside 86
McKay & Blackstock, Messrs 75
Magazine, The 111
Magdalen Fields Golf Club, The 99-100
Main Guard, The 32-33, 79
Maison Dieu 55, 61
Maltings, Pier Road 20
Maps 12, 17, 31, 41, 63, 78, 82, 92, 102, 109, 113
Marlin Buildings 27
Marlin House 27
Married Quarters 7
Martins Printing Works, Messrs 67
Marygate 77-80
Masons Arms, The 95
Meg's Mount 12, 73-76
Merry Wives of Windsor 33
Methodist Chapel, Primitive 90
Monuments 25, 71-72, 86
Moors Bank 72
Mouchel & Partners 66-67
Municipal Buildings 95
Museums 22, 33, 106-107

Nag's Head Inn, The 42
Nelson, Joseph 7
Ness, The 11-12, 16-17
Ness Gate 5-6, 9, 116
Ness Gate Hotel 12
Ness Street 10-12, 14
New Road 64
Newcastle & Berwick Railway 75
Norfolk 20
Northumberland County Council 94-95
Northumbria Healthcare NHS
    Foundation Trust 95

Old Bridge (Berwick Bridge) 56-58, 67
Old Bridge Tavern, The 47
Old Grammar School 13-14, 69
Old Hen & Chickens Inn, The 47
Old Hen & Chickens Public House, The 51
Old Nag's Head Inn, The 42
Old Lifeboat Cottage 27
Old Lifeboat House 27
Old Smoke House 8-9
Ord, William 102
Our Lady & St Cuthbert's Church 72

Painting by Bridge End 61
Palace, the Ness 11, 17, 24-25
Palace, the Castle 24
Palace Green 7, 23-25
Palace Street 24-25, 33
Palace Street East 13-14, 17
Pandora Leaf 80
Parade, The 104
Parish Church of Holy Trinity
    & St Mary 31, 82, 101-102
Paxton & Purves 80
Peacock Inn, The 41
Pennacchini 71
Pennock, William 67
Phillips, Captain Thomas 22, 106
Pictureland (Berwick) Ltd 42
Pier 4-7
Pier Gate 5-6
Pier Road 6, 19-20
Pier Road Malt House 20
Playhouse Cinema 42
Playtime 80
Port Hospital 100
Premier Inn 42
Presbyterian Churches 70-71, 74, 95
Presbyterian Church Manse 31
Primitive Methodist Chapel 90
Prince of Wales (future Edward VIII) 66-67
Prison 74, 94-95
Public convenience, ladies 74-76

Quarries 4-7, 57
Quay Gate 55
Quay Walls [Nos 1-2] 54-55
Quay Walls [Nos 3-5] 52-53
Quay Walls [Nos 6-7] 50-51
Quay Walls [Nos 8-9] 45-47
Quay Walls [Nos 10-14] 43-44
Quay Walls [Nos 15-17] 38-39
Quay Walls [No 18] 36-37
Quay Walls [Nos 19-23] 34-35
Quayside Buildings 44
Quayside Lookout 51

Queen Elizabeth II 90th Birthday 109
Queen Victoria 75-76
Queen Victoria Nurses' Home 47
Queen's Head Hotel, The 42

Rampart House 92
Ravensdale Chapel 60-61, 63
Rawlinson health report [1850] 41, 58, 95-95
Reading Room, Subscription 25
Red Lion Public House 82
Regimental Museum K O Scottish Borderers 106
Rennie, John 7
Reservoir 82
Retreat, The 15-17
Roperies 16, 86, 113
Rowing Club, Berwick-upon-Tweed Amateur 69
Royal Border Bridge 66, 73-76
Royal Tweed Bridge 58, 60, 65-67
Russian cannon 19

St Aidan's House 25, 28-29
St Andrew's Church of Scotland 84, 90, 95
St Andrew's House 90
St Andrew's Place 84
St Bartholomew's Hospital 14
St Edward's Hospital 60-61
St Mary's Church (Medieval) 82
St Mary's Church (Victorian) 82, 102
St Mary Magdalen Hospital 99
St Nicholas' Church 20
Salmon trade 69
Salvation Army 53
Sandgate 40-42
Schofield, Albert 42

School of Industry 29
Schools 13-14, 17, 29, 69, 90
Scots Gate 78
Scout Hall 25
Segate 41
Ship Tavern Public House, The 42
Shipbuilding & Shipbuilders Yard 39
Shore Gate, [Shoregate] 41
Sidey Court 80
Sinclair, George 12
Sinclair, James 12
Skelly & Son, W.R. 80
Smoke House, Old 8-9
Soldiers' Home 37
Specsavers 80
Spittal 7, 14
Spittal Hall Farm 14
Spittal Point 14
Stagecoach Group 66
Statue of Jimmy Strength 25
Stirling, Emily 29
Subscription Reading Room 25
Swimming pool 42
Swimming Race, Bridge-to-Bridge 67

Taffy's Time Machine 80
Theatre 42
Thomas, William 102
Timber yard 5, 9
Tintagel House 60-61, 63-64
Tourist Information Centre 88
Town Guard 32-33
Town Hall 80
Trinitarian friars 60-61

Tweed Brewery 22, 24
Tweedmouth 14, 27, 73-74, 106, 115
Tweedmouth Docks 27

Vaux Brewery 22
Violet Terrace 85-86
Virgin Group 66

Walkergate 80, 90
Wallace Green 93-95
Wallace Green Mission Hall 95
Watchtower Gallery 74
Weatherhead's, solicitors 51
Weatherston, Joseph 84
Wellington bust 25
Wellington Terrace 17, 20, 30-31
Whale Oil House 20
Whaling 20, 31
Wilson, James 7, 25
Wilson Cycles 47
Windmill Bastion 108-109
Windmill Tower 109
Wine and Spirit Museum 22

Young, John 102
Youth & Community Centre 14

Zion Chapel 17, 71